# FROM SOMERSET TO PORTMAN SQUARE
## The Portman Family and their Estates

# FROM SOMERSET TO PORTMAN SQUARE

*The Portman Family and their Estates*

Richard Bowden
*and*
Tom Mayberry

Copyright Richard Bowden and Tom Mayberry © 2022

*All rights reserved*
Unauthorised duplication contravenes existing laws

The right of Richard Bowden and Tom Mayberry to be identified as the authors of this work has been asserted in accordance with the Copyright, Designs and Patents Act 1988

*British Library Cataloguing-in-Publication data*
A catalogue record for this book is available from the British Library

ISBN: 978-1-3999-3256-1

Every effort has been made to trace the copyright holders and obtain permission to reproduce this material.

Designed and typeset by
Carnegie Scotforth Book Production

Printed and bound by Gomer

Frontispiece: Extract from a drawing of Orchard House, Orchard Portman, by James Blackamore, 1774.

# Contents

| | |
|---|---|
| Foreword by *Viscount Portman* | 7 |
| Introduction and Acknowledgements | 9 |
| 1. Origins | 13 |
| 2. Heirs and Successors | 27 |
| 3. The Birth of the London Estate, 1755–1823 | 51 |
| 4. Family Matters | 77 |
| 5. Dorset Days | 93 |
| 6. The Growth of the London Estate, 1824–1919 | 111 |
| 7. The Problems Mount | 131 |
| 8. The Problems Resolved | 153 |
| Appendix: Letter of Richard Norman Shaw, 1889 | 165 |
| Notes and References | 169 |
| Family Trees | 178 |
| Maps | 184 |
| Index | 186 |

Time present and time past
Are both perhaps present in time future,
And time future contained in time past.

> From 'Burnt Norton'
> T. S. Eliot, 1935

# Foreword

It gives me the greatest pleasure to welcome you to this history of the Portman family and their estates. It is 700 years since the Portman family began to make their mark in Somerset, almost 500 years since Sir William Portman took over a lease of land on the edge of London and some 250 years since building began there – so high time for a progress report.

This history was always intended to be a serious (but not too detailed) up-to-date record of what has happened over this long span of time. I am sure you will also agree that the wonderful range of illustrations it includes brings powerfully to life what might otherwise have been a dry chronicle of events.

It is, however, far from that, and a most readable and lively account. It is in many ways an exciting and remarkable story that has renewed my own sense of ancestral admiration and gratitude and which I hope you will enjoy reading.

From the market stall in Taunton recorded soon after 1300, followed by a succession of lawyers and MPs, to the estate's recent involvement in the process of modernising Baker Street and the traffic flow in London's West End, a continuous theme in our history has been working with and for the local community.

The family's former homes at Orchard Portman and Bryanston are now part of our history – the Portman family and their estates will always be remembered in Somerset and Dorset. But our 'home' is now in London, where I hope we shall continue to make a major contribution for many years to come.

Christopher Portman<br>
10th Viscount Portman

# Introduction and Acknowledgements

The idea for this new history of the Portman family emerged from a visit made to the West Country by the trustees of The Portman Estate. The last of the Portman lands in Somerset and Dorset were sold in the 1950s, but the trustees were impressed by how rich a legacy the family had left in their old home territory. It was decided that a new history should be written, tracing the family's long journey from their Somerset origins to the heart of the capital city.

Many existing works of scholarship illuminate the history of the Portmans. Thomas Smith's pioneering history of Marylebone was published in 1833 and Gordon Mackenzie's *Marylebone* in 1972. *Marylebone & Tyburn Past*, by David Brandon and Alan Brooke, appeared in 2007 and there are literally hundreds of other works on relevant aspects of London. West Country studies are fewer. They include histories of individual Portman parishes by Sir Matthew Nathan and Rosemary Sixsmith, M. J. Hawkins's article on seventeenth-century Portmans published in 1982 and Susan Moore's unpublished history of Bryanston completed in 1993. Marjorie Portman's *Bryanston: Picture of a Family*, published in 1987, is particularly valuable for its personal recollections, and Tom Mayberry's *Orchard and the Portmans*, from 1986, seeks briefly to tell the family's Somerset story. Some of its contents are drawn on in this book.

The Portman archives in London and Somerset have been a fundamental historical source. By the time plans for the book were taking shape Richard Bowden had been appointed Archives Consultant for the Estate and had begun work on cataloguing the collection now preserved in the estate office at Portman Square. Records of the once vast estates have been considerably reduced by office moves and a succession of property sales. They were also greatly affected by the Second World War. In October 1938, at the time of the Munich crisis, Captain Gerald Portman, who then managed the London and Dorset estates, wrote to his agent, Mr Furmedge:

> I fear the dwellers in town and especially London must have had an anxious time the past 10 days. I was wondering whether I hadn't better come down and arrange to move the Estate Office to the country! But I didn't see how it could be done.

His fears were well founded. On 8 December 1940 the estate office at 111 Baker Street all but disappeared in a bombing raid, with the loss of unknown quantities of records. Captain Portman, who was in Scotland at the time, immediately agreed that the office should be moved to Montagu House, the family's London home in Portman Square. Then on the night of 10–11 May 1941 Montagu House was itself gutted by fire bombs. No one was hurt, and the archives, stored in an inner cellar, survived the destruction. They were soon sent to Dorset for safekeeping and some were even microfilmed. Captain Portman's particular concern at this moment of crisis was not for the archives but the paintings, especially George Stubbs's 'The Royal Tiger'. But Mr Furmedge was able to reassure him by telegram that 'the Tiger is safely caged in Dorset'.

In creating the book Richard Bowden has been chiefly responsible for the London chapters and Tom Mayberry chiefly for the West Country chapters. Both have contributed to the many aspects of a lengthy and complex project and are indebted to all those who have so generously given help. They include members of the Portman family and several present and former members of the Estate staff.

Particular thanks are due to Lt Commander Simon Emmet, Kellie Heber-Percy, Viscount and the late Viscountess Knutsford, The Hon. Mrs Rosemary Pease, Lt Col. Michael Portman, The Hon. Claire Robinson, Lady Thompson, Charlotte Alexander, the late Tony Brock, Mireille Galinou, the late Frank Gibson, James Gibson Fleming, Charles Hatherell, Brenda Hill, Andrea Hinks, Conrad Keating, Richard Lay,

Alan Shrimpton, Joyce Slaymaker, Isobel Watson, Rachel Hunt and Sarah Charlton, the Estate's Archivist. John Tory drew attention to the diaries of Julietta Forrester, 1856–1917, and Jeremy Drax, their owner, has kindly given permission for them to be used. John Tory's selected transcript of the diaries has proved an invaluable way into this remarkable record of life on the Bryanston estate. Sabera Bham was very helpful concerning illustrations as were the staffs of Westminster City Archives, the South West Heritage Trust and Somerset Archaeological and Natural History Society. At the estate office Henrietta Cohen skilfully coordinated the gathering of the illustrations.

Finally, thanks must go to Katie Balderson, the Estate Secretary, who has been outstandingly supportive during the long gestation of this history and has guided it to publication with great patience and care.

Richard Bowden
Tom Mayberry

*A Note on Money Values.* It is difficult to give modern equivalents for the historic money values used in this book, especially those from more distant periods. As an approximate guide, £1 in 1750 was worth about £211 in 2017; £1 in 1850 was worth about £128 in 2017; and £1 in 1950 was worth about £33 in 2017.

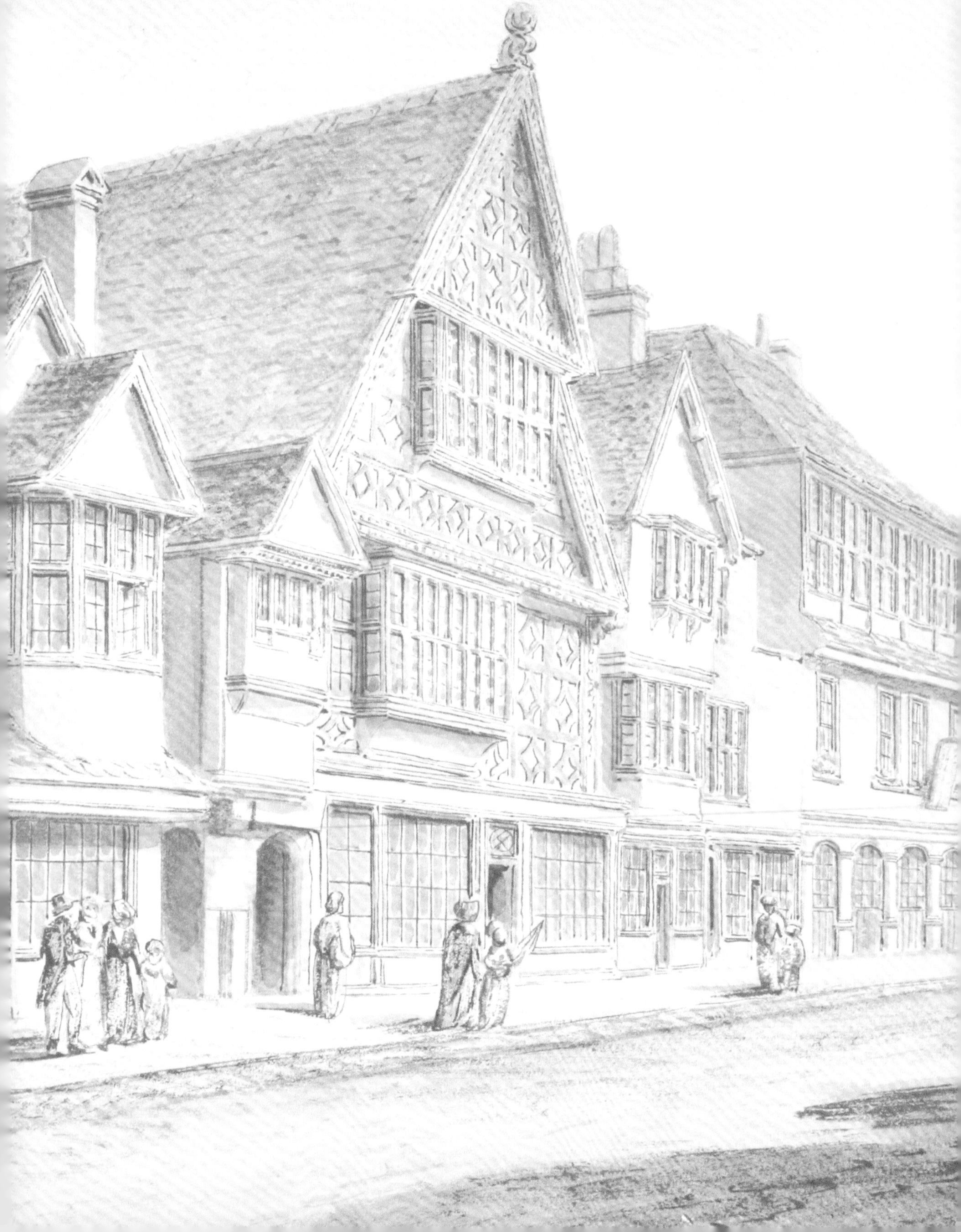

CHAPTER 1
# Origins

*Rural Roots*

The Somerset town of Taunton was a large and prosperous borough in the late Middle Ages. Its fine parish church, St Mary Magdalene, stood as a proud expression of merchant wealth and religious faith, while close by, at the meeting point of the town's three main streets, a large market place formed Taunton's commercial centre. This cobbled triangular space contained market standings, a guildhall and many inns, and was bounded along its three sides by the houses of merchants and wealthier tradesmen. It was in this bustling provincial setting, far from London, that the story of the Portman family begins.

Taunton lies at the heart of the great Vale of Taunton Deane, an area long famed for its beauty and agricultural fertility. The town, and the wider landscape around it, were given by Anglo-Saxon kings to the bishops of Winchester in the tenth century and later. And although in 1135 King Stephen granted Taunton the privileges of a borough, the power of the bishops, whose castle stood just outside the borough boundary, would shape the town's history for hundreds of years.[1]

It is likely, though not certain, that the origins of the Portman family were located in or near Taunton. A 'portman' or 'portreeve' was a leading citizen of a borough, one of the select group entrusted with its government.[2] It would be no surprise if the family which later showed such legal and commercial ability had already achieved a leading role in the life of the town at an early date. But only in the fourteenth century do the Portmans emerge in the written record. In 1301–2 'Thomas the Portman' appears in a transaction relating to property in Taunton, and in 1307–8 he rented a standing in the market place for 10*d.* a year. By 1334–5 the family held at least 12 messuages, or dwellings, in the town, and in the early fifteenth century became owners of the house in Fore

The medieval church of St Mary Magdalene, Taunton, *c.* 1780. Early members of the Portman family were baptised and married there. Taunton Priory, where some of them were buried, stood nearby.
*Image: Somerset Archaeological and Natural History Society*

'Ancient houses in Fore Street, Taunton.' Watercolour by J. C. Buckler, 1832. The high-gabled building in the centre was the house acquired by the Portman family early in the 15th century. Tradition says that Sir William Portman, 6th baronet, entertained Judge Jeffreys there during the Bloody Assizes in 1685.
*Image: Somerset Archaeological and Natural History Society*

Street whose later half-timbered façade is still one of Taunton's most striking historic features.³

The earliest member of the Portman family to leave a substantial record was probably born in the 1330s, and like so many who came after him was called William. He served as Taunton's Member of Parliament on eleven occasions between 1362 and 1406 and grew prosperous as a merchant. There is evidence that he may have traded in wine, but like his fellow Taunton MP, William Marchaunt, he probably owed much of his success to the woollen-cloth trade that dominated the economy both of Taunton and of Somerset as a whole.

By the time this William Portman was buried at Taunton Priory in about 1413, his son Walter was already established as a lawyer, the profession in which the family would achieve its rapid rise to prominence

St Michael's Church, Orchard Portman. Watercolour by J. Buckler, 1832. The aisle in the foreground, demolished in 1844, was the burial place of the de Orchard family.
*Image: Somerset Archaeological and Natural History Society*

during the next three generations. Walter, like his father, was often chosen as Taunton's MP, and between 1417 and 1435 sat in ten parliaments. His evident skill in the law gained him powerful friends. He advised the Luttrells of Dunster Castle when their title to the Dunster estates was questioned; and on another occasion he acted in a land transaction for Sir John Stourton, later Treasurer of the royal household. But perhaps nothing in Walter's life exceeded in importance his marriage, by 1440, to a Somerset widow called Christina de Orchard.[4]

Christina was heiress to a landowning family which had been settled near Taunton since at least the twelfth century. In about 1158 her ancestor, Richard de Orchard, was tenant of the manor called Orchard, and may well have been living when a splendid twelfth-century doorway, which survives today, was added to the parish church. Walter's marriage to Christina brought him modest landed wealth of a kind that the Portmans had previously lacked, and gave substance to the gentry status implied by his new coat of arms. The arms showed a blue fleur de lis on a yellow ground and have remained in use by the Portmans ever since.

Walter's son John followed him into the law, and when in the 1460s he wrote home to 'hys Ryght Worshypfull Moder' in a rare surviving letter, it was from the Temple in London that he addressed her. His own son, another John, achieved distinction as a lawyer in his turn and was buried in the Temple Church in 1521. But it was in the following generation, above all, that ability and opportunity were most strikingly matched.[5]

## Making a Name

Sir William Portman (*c.* 1498–1557) was son of John the younger, and in 1517 entered the Middle Temple like his father before him. Sir William was evidently a man of outstanding gifts. Having become a serjeant-at-law in 1540, he was made a judge of King's Bench in 1546, was knighted the following year, and in 1555 reached the top of his profession as Lord Chief Justice. He steered a safe course through the religious changes of his age, faithful as a Protestant in Edward VI's reign, and as a Catholic in Queen Mary's. Nor did he neglect the opportunities available to men of his class to profit from the flourishing land market following the dissolution of the monasteries. 'Horner, Paget, Portman, Thynne,' went one version of a local rhyme. 'When the monks stepped out you stepped in.'

It was in 1544 that Sir William acquired estates belonging to four of Somerset's dissolved religious houses, among them Taunton Priory and Athelney Abbey. His new possessions included the manors of North Petherton, Clavelshays, Durleigh, Goathurst and Dunwear, together with land in fourteen other places. These estates were added to existing holdings in Orchard Portman, Bickenhall, Taunton and elsewhere, and rapidly made the Portman family one of the greatest landowners in the West Country. But the Lord Chief Justice's most significant purchase took place far from Somerset when, in 1532, he acquired

Portrait of Sir William Portman (c. 1498–1557), appointed Lord Chief Justice in 1555. The portrait is thought to have been painted in the 17th century.
*Image: The Portman Estate*

a substantial farming estate in the fields of Marylebone. By the late eighteenth century those fields were being developed as one of London's most fashionable districts, and by the late nineteenth century had made the Portmans among the richest ground landlords in England.[6]

When Sir William died in 1557, he left instructions for a funeral 'withoute pompe and pride'. But such a wish was unlikely to be granted to someone who had risen so high. Instead his London funeral, at St Dunstan's in the West, Fleet Street, was marked by lavish ceremony. The heraldry displayed for the occasion included a leopard's head in gold with two snakes coming out of its mouth. There were mantles of black velvet, four 'grett gylt candylstykes' and two dozen torches; and in the procession that followed the Chief Justice to his grave were six judges

View of Orchard House, Orchard Portman. Oil by Leonard Knyff, c. 1705. The house sits in the midst of farmland, avenues of trees and formal gardens. The parish church is in the foreground.
*Image: Royal Collection Trust / © Her Majesty Queen Elizabeth II 2018*

and all the inns of court. The following day, to conclude the ceremonies, three 'goodly masses' were sung, and a sermon was preached.[7]

The family's horizons widened rapidly from the sixteenth century onwards, but their home, and the centre of their influence, remained in Somerset. Orchard House, finally demolished in about 1844, was the visible expression of their status, and at its greatest extent was one of the most remarkable houses in the West Country. Little is known of the medieval house of the de Orchards, from which the later mansion presumably developed: an account roll for 1347–8 mentions a 'hall with chambers and other rooms', a dovecote and a watermill, a garden of six acres, and a church worth £10 a year.[8] By contrast, Orchard House, as it developed during the sixteenth century, is extensively recorded in watercolours and sketches, as well as in Leonard Knyff's painting of about 1705.

Knyff's painting, and the engraving by Johannes Kip derived from it, have long been thought to show a many-gabled Tudor house overshadowed by the enormous three-sided courtyard of a new 17th-century building. But the recent discovery of four drawings, made by James Blackamore in 1773–4, leads to a different and more interesting conclusion. The drawings suggest that the gabled building was only a little earlier in date than the courtyard range, and was possibly the work of John Portman, father of the Lord Chief Justice. The courtyard range, whose windows as shown by Blackamore were evidently of about 1540, may have been the grandly ambitious work of the Lord Chief Justice himself. If so, its symmetrical plan and shallow roofs, hidden behind balustraded parapets, are remarkable evidence for the early influence of the Renaissance in England, and make Orchard House a building of outstanding interest. The mansion's very innovative design may also suggest that the Lord Chief Justice had travelled in Europe. The interior of the house is difficult to evoke, though a detailed inventory of 1690 refers to the hall, the parlour, the long gallery and the oriel, together with chambers of yellow, grey, purple and blue.[9]

The Lord Chief Justice's immediate successors did not achieve his degree of national prominence. They were content to serve locally as Justices of the Peace and to be elected to Parliament with fair regularity. But surviving records reflect most of all their activities as landowners. Sir Henry Portman (d. 1591), son of the Chief Justice, added almost 1,000 acres in Thurloxton to the estate, as well as lands in Puckington, Pilton, East Chinnock and Closworth. The acquisitions of Henry's own sons, Sir Hugh (d. 1604) and Sir John (d. 1612), included the manor of Staple Fitzpaine, land at Kew on which Kew Palace would later rise and much

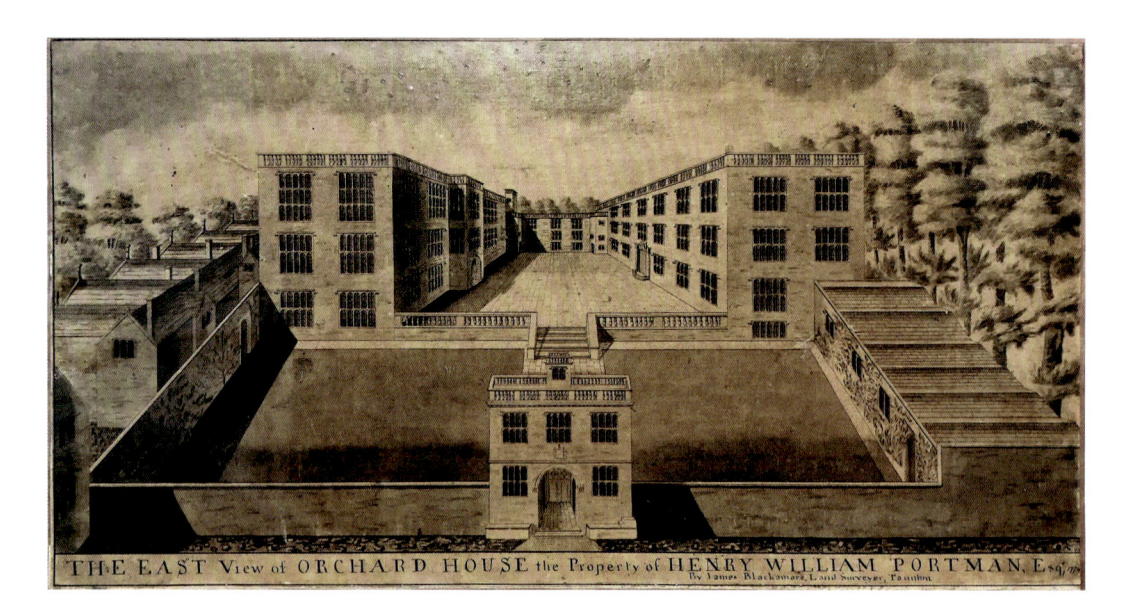

THE EAST View of ORCHARD HOUSE the Property of HENRY WILLIAM PORTMAN, Esq.
By James Blackamore, Land surveyor, Taunton

Orchard House, Orchard Portman, seen from the east. Drawing by James Blackamore, 1774. The courtyard range seen here was demolished soon afterwards, the remainder of the house in about 1844.
*Image: South West Heritage Trust*

land in and near West Coker, where Sir John's 'exquisitely beautiful' manor house survives. In 1616 the Portmans also acquired the site of Muchelney Abbey, near Langport, together with the beautiful abbot's lodgings. In the course of the seventeenth century the Somerset estate grew to include most of the 24,000 acres it still contained two hundred years later.[10]

The Portmans added to their status not just as landowners. In 1611 Sir John Portman paid £1,095 to obtain a baronetcy, a hereditary honour that descended in his family for the next 80 years, and the marriages of his children linked the Portmans to some of the West Country's leading families. His eldest daughter Joan (1598–1655) married George Speke of Whitelackington, and his youngest child, Anne (1610–1695), was the wife of Sir Edward Seymour. When Elizabeth (1604–1636) married John Bluett of Holcombe Rogus, Devon, she became mistress of one of the West Country's finest houses; and after they died a splendid tomb was made for them which includes the kneeling figures of their eight children.[11]

It is in death as well that we discover her brother Sir John Portman (1605–1624), the 3rd baronet. He died at the age of only 19 while a student at Wadham College, Oxford. But his name lives on through his fine monument in the college chapel.[12]

Monument in All Saints Church, Holcombe Rogus, Devon, to John Bluett and his wife Elizabeth (d. 1636), daughter of Sir John Portman, 1st baronet. In the pediment of the tomb the Bluett arms are impaled with the Portman fleur de lis.

*Image: Tom Mayberry*

Monument to Sir John Portman (1605–1624), 3rd baronet, in the chapel of Wadham College, Oxford. The monument includes Sir John's reclining effigy as well as figures of Time and four virtues.
*Image: Tom Mayberry*

## Civil War

If the Portmans by the early seventeenth century were chiefly content to grow great as landowners, and to ally themselves by marriage to other leading West County families, they were not left undisturbed to enjoy their prosperity. They lived in times too troubled and demanding for that to be possible, and much too close to Taunton. That this was the case found expression most of all in the brief and tragic life of another Sir William Portman (1608–1645), the youngest son of the 1st baronet. He succeeded his three short-lived brothers to become 5th baronet in 1629, and by the time of his death at the close of the first Civil War, his home and his family had passed through the most dramatic period in their history.

When the Civil War broke out in 1642 there was no town more willing than Taunton to support the cause of Parliament, and none more estranged from the policies of the king. The clothworking townsmen resented King Charles's attempts to extract arbitrary taxation from them in the form of Ship Money and preferred Puritan religion to the Anglicanism of Archbishop Laud. Only gradually did Sir William Portman decide where his own loyalties and interests lay. As High

Sheriff of Somerset in 1637–8 he served the king well in the collection of Ship Money, but by 1642 he was at the head of a Parliamentary force in control of Taunton. He had evidently not abandoned hope of the godly reformation in church and state that he and fellow members of the Long Parliament had been striving for. But the radical divide which outright war soon created convinced him that it was with the king, after all, that he should stand. Sir William Portman would die a Royalist.[13]

It was not surprising that his mansion found a place in the events that now so dramatically affected Taunton. The house first saw action during 1643. In June that year a Royalist force under Sir Ralph Hopton, Lord Hertford and Prince Maurice briefly made headquarters there during the campaign that established the king's supremacy in Somerset. On the morning after their arrival they advanced on Taunton, over 6,000 strong, and the Parliamentary garrison retreated 'in great hast' towards Bridgwater. But victory that day endured for little more than a year. In July 1644 the town was recaptured for Parliament from a depleted garrison and was made an island of Parliamentary resistance once more. When, in due course, the Royalists responded to their loss of Taunton with a series of bitter sieges, no one forgot the usefulness of Orchard House as a last staging-post on the road to town.[14]

It was Richard Batt, Sir William's steward, who carried much of the responsibility for defending his master's interests in the troubled times ahead. In later years he would recall how, at some time before the first siege of Taunton began, £200 in silver was hidden in the gallery at Orchard House. It disappeared forever shortly afterwards when 'the same gallery with the whole howse there became…full of soldiers and a garrison made thereof'. In the events that followed Batt recorded that the mansion served by turns as headquarters for the Royalist and Parliamentary armies, 'and beinge made garryson gave entertainment and quarters to both the said armies souldery'.[15]

The first to arrive there were the Royalist forces commanded by Colonel Edmund Wyndham who laid siege to Taunton in October 1644. Wyndham's forces attacked repeatedly, but the offer of honourable surrender terms brought only blunt defiance from Robert Blake, the Parliamentary commander in Taunton. 'We neither feare your menaces nor accept your proferrs,' Blake wrote in a letter sent to Wyndham 'at his quarters at Orchard'. Not for the last time, Blake's courage was vindicated, and early in December Wyndham marched away having learnt that a Parliamentary relief force was approaching. When those rescuers at last reached Taunton on 14 December, they took over Wyndham's headquarters, and next day Sir Anthony Ashley Cooper wrote from Orchard to the Earl of Essex describing Taunton's survival as 'almost a miracle'.[16]

Of the Portmans themselves in these months, little is known, though it is clear they did not stray far from home. A note in the Orchard Portman parish register records that on 10 September 1644 'my Lady Anne Portman was delivered of her first borne sonne…between 9 and 10 at night', and on 26 September, days before the first siege began, the child was brought for baptism in the parish church. He was called William, like the father he would hardly know, and was destined to earn a lasting place in the history of his times. But the circumstances of his first months could hardly have given less cause for hopefulness. The great house was filled with soldiers, Taunton was under siege, and the fortunes of Sir William Portman were fast ebbing away.

More loyal to home territory than was safe in such a crisis, Sir William had become Blake's prisoner in Taunton by February 1645, and so was a witness at first hand to the town's terrible sufferings when the Royalist siege was renewed in March. Without friends or money, Sir William was forced to borrow £40 from one of Blake's garrison, money which was evidently demanded by the borough constable to pay for 'fire and candles for the guard during the sieges'.[17]

While Sir William remained trapped in Taunton, his mansion was again made headquarters for the Royalists as the second siege began. Now, however, the gentlemanly Colonel Wyndham was replaced by General Goring and Sir Richard Grenville, both ruthlessly determined men whose ill-disciplined troops were soon accused of terrible acts of 'plunder and rapine'. Not until 11 May 1645, after at least a third of the town had been reduced to ashes, did a Parliamentary relief force reach Taunton, bringing 'unspeakable comfort to the distressed inhabitants'. But the suffering was not quite at an end. In June, Goring blockaded Taunton in the hope that it could be starved into submission. Then, in early July, he abandoned the struggle and marched away, his deserted quarters at Orchard yielding large quantities of wheat which supplied a 'great market' held in Taunton.[18]

The final stages of Sir William Portman's tragedy were now quickly played out. Rising above a character remembered on one occasion as 'very various and uncertain', he evidently made his escape from Taunton at the end of the second siege in May. On 14 June 1645 he was among some dozen former Royalist members of the Long Parliament who fought for King Charles at the Battle of Naseby and shared that day in the decisive defeat of Royalist hopes. With Sir Henry Vaughan, former member for Carmarthen, Sir William was carried prisoner to London, and on 20 June he appeared at the bar of the House of Commons to face the colleagues who, eighteen months before, had expelled him as a Royalist delinquent. Exactly what happened that day is not recorded. We know only that Sir William was committed to the Tower of London, and that on 20 August he died there, 'a prisoner for loyalty'. Special leave of the House was required before he could be carried home to Orchard Portman, the parish register recording that on 22 September he was finally 'interred with his ancestors in his vault in Orchard Church'.[19]

Sir William's mansion, the inheritance of a child scarcely one year old, stood desolate after the months of military occupation, and soon it had been made a 'pesthowse for the infected people of the towne of Taunton'. Vital deeds and documents of the estate had been rifled and dispersed, and it seems likely that even the church plate had been plundered. The Portman family, in a gesture of striking magnanimity, gave the parish church a new chalice and cover after the Civil War, engraved with the Portman fleur-de-lis and bearing the date letter for 1646. That gift, and the almshouses which Sir William founded at Staple Fitzpaine in 1643, are some memorial to the baronet and his family in the years of their greatest trouble.[20]

Chalice and cover presented by the Portmans to St Michael's Church, Orchard Portman, following the Civil War. They bear the date letter for 1646.
*Image: St Michael's Church, Orchard Portman*

The Orchard is well

wasth to plan

Roockery
Trees here and
behind the Bowling
Greene

Mr Shawn
Morley

yard

Church

Bowling
Greene

Dove
House

Pound

Garden

CHAPTER 2

# Heirs and Successors

## *The Last Baronet*

The price of fighting for a losing cause had been very high and was not yet fully paid even with the death of the 5th baronet. Until January 1649 the Portman estates were sequestered by Parliament, and a delinquency fine of over £6,000 was imposed on the family and given in recompense to the people of Taunton. It was later estimated that the Portmans lost £30,000 as a result of the war. But to a family whose landed wealth was so great, even that financial catastrophe soon appeared no more than a temporary setback. While the new Sir William Portman (1644–1690), a sickly and probably consumptive youth, was being taught to dance and play the viol under the care of his uncle, his trustees found themselves controlling an income so large that they were able to acquire new lands in Dorset. By 1662 the great mansion and estate at Bryanston near Blandford Forum was in Portman ownership, and in 1682 other lands near Orchard Portman itself were acquired.[1]

The brief but remarkable life of the 6th baronet saw the Portmans flourish as never before. At the coronation of Charles II in 1661, Sir William, aged only sixteen, was made a Knight of the Bath, and the same year renewed his family's sometimes uneasy political links with Taunton when he was elected member for the town. In 1664 he became one of the early fellows of the Royal Society and probably

Portrait miniature of Sir William Portman (1644–1690), 6th baronet, as a young man.
*Image: ©Victoria and Albert Museum, London*

counted the scientists Edmund Halley and Robert Hooke among his close friends, as his steward Thomas Axe certainly did. John Evelyn, the diarist, pictures Sir William one day in 1680 dining with Lady Mordaunt and Samuel Pepys, and there can be little doubt that as one of the most powerful men in the West of England he moved easily among the greatest in the land.[2]

In politics his loyalty to the Tories, the court party, could usually be depended on. There was never danger, at least, that he would follow his more radical cousins the Spekes and side with the Whigs, opponents of the court. His private character remains obscure, but we may certainly allow him his contemporary reputation for great charity. By the late 1680s he was making substantial annual gifts in money and food to the Taunton poor, and at his death left £90 a year for apprenticing eighteen children from the town and elsewhere. 'We all know that Sir W[illiam] P[ortman] is so noble a spirit', it was remarked, 'that the absolute poor do not use to want what he has.' Perhaps the ill-health he suffered throughout his life, and three childless if

Arms of the Portman family quartered with the arms of Trivett, de Orchard, Crosse, Maningford and Gilbert. They were carved during the seventeenth century and probably formed part of a chimney-piece at Orchard House.
*Image: Tom Mayberry*

profitable marriages, had tempered ambition and made his a more than conventional charity.[3]

His first wife, Elizabeth Cutler, died in 1673, his second, Elizabeth Southcote, in 1680, and his third, Mary Holman, in 1689, fourteen months before Sir William himself. His household at Orchard Portman included a numerous band of other relatives and retainers. The Revd Thomas Lessey, domestic chaplain to the 'priest-ridden' baronet, stood high among this privileged group, as did Thomas Axe, who served him for more than 30 years. There was room as well for Sir William's swashbuckling kinsman, Captain Humphrey Colles, who in 1662 'fought strenuously against the Moors…in the field of Tangier', while in the kitchens presided Mr Stollar the cook, preparing a swan for his master's table one day in 1684.[4]

A wide net of family relationships brought others to Orchard House in the Restoration period. The political intriguer Hugh Speke of Whitelackington, son of Sir William's cousin George Speke, must have been a frequent if sometimes unwelcome caller. Another cousin, the great Sir Edward Seymour of Maiden Bradley, was certainly well known at the gate, and was one of the few West Country Tories to whose power and prestige Sir William need defer. Samuel Pepys found Seymour 'mighty high', but his ability was quite the equal of his notorious pride, and he served as the most distinguished Speaker of the Restoration House of Commons. Seymour's presence at Orchard confirms the mansion's continuing role as a political focus in the later seventeenth century. Just as in the Civil War, it was Taunton, ever troublesome, which made that role inevitable.[5]

## *The Monmouth Rebellion*

No more loyal to King Charles II than they had been to his father, the people of Taunton joyfully celebrated 11 May each year as the day of their deliverance from the Royalist siege of 1645, and showed their opinion of the re-established Anglican Church by flocking in their hundreds to nonconformist conventicles. In July 1665, two justices and a body of Sir William's servants went brandishing swords to break up a great conventicle at the home of a Taunton merchant called John Mallack. The famous preacher Joseph Alleine was Mallack's house guest, and it was at a meeting intended as his farewell that the unwelcome visitors from Orchard House now arrived. They broke down the doors, 'though they might have unlatched them if they had pleased', and after much 'deriding and menacing' of those present, handed them over to the constables.[6]

West Country people viewed with alarm the probable succession to the throne of the king's Catholic brother, James, Duke of York. Their hopes lay instead with Charles's illegitimate son, the Duke of Monmouth. When Monmouth, hero of the Whigs, made a grand tour of the region in 1680, public enthusiasm knew no bounds. He even felt confident of a welcome at Orchard House as he set out on the road from London. But in the event he avoided the Vale of Taunton altogether and settled for the hospitality of others, including Sir William Portman's bad-tempered Whig cousin, George Speke.[7]

Monmouth's expectations of Sir William himself were ill-founded. The independently-minded baronet had no intention of throwing in his lot with Monmouth and the Whigs, his chaplain reporting of him in 1679 that although he opposed Catholicism he remained 'firm to king and church'. By 1681 Sir William, like many of his class, had struck a delicate balance between conscience and pragmatism and was said to be drinking the health of the Catholic Duke of York. Two years later he was loyally searching for arms and interrogating malcontents on suspicion of a planned uprising in Taunton. And when in 1685 Monmouth's rebel army finally began to march, no one was more ready to serve the new King James than Sir William Portman.[8]

Sir William was attending Parliament when rumours of a planned rebellion reached their height during late May and early June 1685. It was Thomas Axe, his steward, who found himself in sole charge at Orchard House in the eye of the growing storm, and who gave warning to his master in a series of letters sent to London. Their contents, it seems likely, immediately reached the king. On 30 May, Axe forwarded to Sir William a copy of an intercepted letter addressed to a Taunton man which left no doubt that Monmouth's landing from the Continent was expected soon. Two days later followed news of 80 horsemen seen riding in the night, and by 3 June Axe could report the fears of a member of Taunton corporation that 'some wicked designe' was afoot.

Early on the morning of Friday 12 June, a messenger arrived at Orchard House 'almost out of breath' to bring news of Monmouth's landing at Lyme Regis. A servant from the house, perhaps Axe himself, immediately rode south to spy out the enemy's strength and returned at two o'clock the following morning to report to the waiting household. The same day Sir William Portman and Colonel Strangways hastened to the West Country with orders from the king to take charge of the militia. Sir William arrived at Bryanston 'very sick', but struggled on that night as far as Dorchester where the Yellow Regiment of the Dorset militia awaited him. On 14 June he led them into Bridport before noon and shortly afterwards took possession of Lyme Regis. But he was not destined quite yet to face the Duke of Monmouth. Already the rebels had marched onward from Lyme, gaining rapidly in numbers as they went.[9]

Chard was reached on 16 June, Ilminster the following day, and on 18 June they made for Taunton itself, 'the sink of all the rebellion in the West'. As they approached the town some rebels stopped at Orchard House in search of arms and horses. It was useless for Axe and his fellow servants to resist, and the army continued on its triumphant way the better by the contents of Sir William's armoury and stables. On 27 June at Norton St Philip Monmouth's rebels resisted attack by a royal army which included Sir William Portman. But on 6 July at the Battle of Sedgemoor they were utterly defeated.[10]

The last of the battle was still being fought as Monmouth made his escape over the Polden Hills, accompanied by Lord Grey, his second-in-command, and Anton Buyse, a German artilleryman. They sheltered first at Downside, then rode south-east into Dorset, hoping to find a boat on the coast near Poole or Lymington to carry them beyond the king's reach. Lord Lumley's Sussex militia were already searching on the western borders of Hampshire, well aware that Monmouth might choose to flee that way. At the same time Sir William Portman had posted his yellow coats and others to form a line of watches reaching from Poole to the far north of Dorset.[11]

At Cranbourne Chase the fugitives abandoned their horses and, dressing themselves in country clothes, continued on foot towards the coast. Lord Grey was the first to be taken. He had decided to separate from his companions, and on the morning of 7 July was discovered on the Dorset side of Ringwood by some of Lumley's troops. Certain that the Duke himself was not far distant, Lumley ordered a search of the cottages scattered over the heathy district, and Sir William Portman hastened in to assist with as many horse and foot as he could muster. At last the pursuers closed on an area at Horton near Ringwood where the land was divided into many small fields and stood like an island surrounded by the heath. A poor cottager called Amy Farrant admitted that she had seen two men clamber over a hedge there, though tradition adds that she wished ever after she had kept her secret.

Monmouth and Buyse tried in vain to elude the troops who beat through the fields till darkness fell, and after midnight, when the baying of the bloodhounds had died away, Monmouth lay down in a ditch by an ash tree and slept a free man for the last time. At first light the

Engraving showing the capture of the Duke of Monmouth by Sir William Portman, 8 July 1685.
*Image: Somerset Archaeological and Natural History Society*

soldiers pressed in once more, and at 5 o'clock Buyse was taken. But two more hours passed before one Henry Parkin found the sleeping Monmouth hidden beneath a covering of ferns and bracken. Two Sussex troopers were called to assist, and soon afterwards Sir William Portman rode in to silence the cries of 'Shoot him, shoot him!' that were already being raised. 'He laid hands on him as his prisoner', a contemporary account records, 'and so preserv'd him from all violence and rudeness.'

If Sir William was inclined to view that moment as a personal triumph, he cannot have failed to recognise its tragedy as well. The man on whom so many hopes had rested now shook uncontrollably from hunger and fatigue as he faced his captor under the Dorset sky, and dressed in 'an old frize-coat, and a mean hat', was hardly recognisable as the brilliant courtier Sir William must have known well. When Lumley reached the scene moments later, it was agreed that Sir William should search the Duke, and there, with a pocketful of guineas, a book of charms, songs and prayers, and a treatise on fortification, was found his 'George', part of the insignia of a garter knight given by King Charles to his favourite son over twenty years before. The George was dispatched to London as proof of Monmouth's capture, while Lumley and Sir William escorted the Duke himself by slower stages to the capital. The formality of a trial was unnecessary for a proclaimed traitor, and any hope of mercy was soon abandoned. On 15 July 1685, before a great and silent crowd on Tower Hill, the Protestant Duke was beheaded.

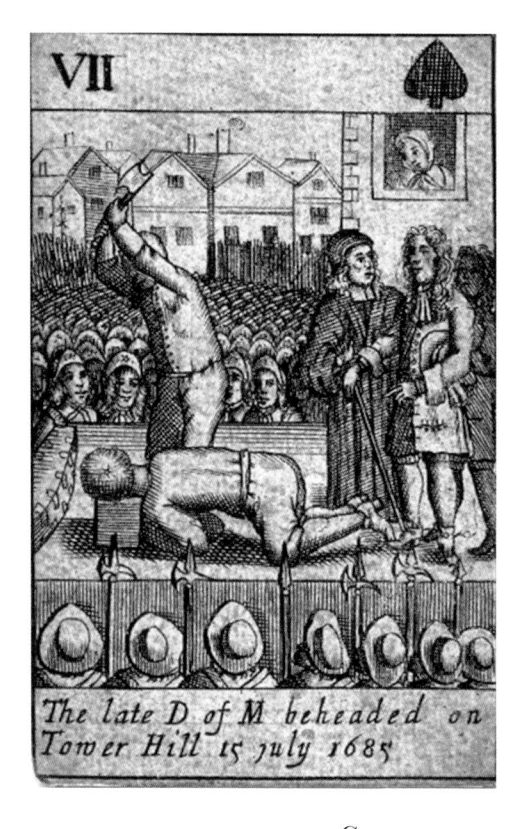

Contemporary playing card showing the execution of the Duke of Monmouth on Tower Hill, London, 15 July 1685.
*Image: The British Library*

## Aftermath

People of all classes in the West Country were appalled by the Bloody Assizes, King James's brutal answer to his rebellious subjects. Sir William's young cousin Charles Speke was hanged at Ilminster for no greater crime than shaking Monmouth's hand, and throughout the countryside the quartered remains of other victims were displayed in gruesome warning.

Soon, the autocratic rule of the Catholic king had alienated even loyal Tories, and when, in November 1688, a ship bearing the Prince of Orange arrived at Brixham, Sir William Portman was soon at the Prince's side, helping to forge what history calls the Glorious Revolution.[12]

Any who feared that this enterprise would end as Monmouth's had were soon reassured. The Whig gentry of Devon overcame their initial caution, and after careful thought West Country Tories also decided in favour of the Prince, influenced most by Sir Edward Seymour. On 17 November 1688 Sir Edward, together with his cousin Sir William Portman and other Tory gentlemen, set off on the road to Exeter and joined the Prince in the city that night. Next day it was Seymour who proposed the 'Exeter Association', a document pledging that the disparate band now gathering to the Prince would unite to uphold his cause and strive until the kingdom was 'no more in danger of falling under popery and slavery'.[13]

While Seymour was left behind as governor of Exeter, Sir William marched with the Prince towards London, and was at his side as the army advanced from Mere to Salisbury. By 12 December, the day after King James had fled from London and effectively ended his reign, Sir William was home once more at Orchard. There he busily attempted to raise a loan for the Prince and speculated perhaps on the advancement which must surely be his reward under the new regime. But just when the most important years of his political life seemed before him illness returned, and by 19 December Sir William had taken to his bed, too weak even to write.[14]

He found strength enough to stand for election at Taunton that winter. The campaign was a boisterous one, the Whigs complaining that they had been set upon by the Portman camp and that a riot had been started at the hustings by Sir William's coachman and huntsman. Sir William was duly returned as a member for the town, rewarding those who supported him with a feast and a shilling each (or so it was claimed by the Whig losers). But he would take no part in the momentous Convention Parliament which soon gathered in London and offered the throne to William and Mary as joint sovereigns. Sir William's health was broken, and even the attentions of Thomas Millington and Richard Lower, two of the leading physicians of the day, could do little.[15]

As his life ebbed away Sir William's chief preoccupation was to ensure the future of his name and lands. He had no children to succeed him and his nearest heirs were now his cousins, including George Speke, Sir Edward Seymour and Sir Edward's youngest brother Henry. All were the grandchildren of Sir John Portman, the 1st baronet. Sir William decided that Henry Seymour should succeed him, and that

Monument by Michael Rysbrack in All Saints Church, Maiden Bradley, Wiltshire, to Sir Edward Seymour (1633–1708). He was Speaker of the House of Commons and cousin of Sir William Portman, 6th baronet. *Image: Tom Mayberry*

if Henry in turn died childless the estate should then pass to William Berkeley, another descendant of Sir John's.

During February and March 1690, Sir William drew up his will and the settlement deeds that would give effect to his decision – a decision that would have far-reaching consequences. A later legal case provides vivid details of the process and of Sir William's last anxious weeks at Orchard House. The will and settlement were prepared by Thomas Axe, and on 9 March, the day they were signed and sealed, Sir William sent servants repeatedly to Axe's chamber to hasten the work. Finally, as night approached, Sir William's neighbour, George Musgrave, and other witnesses, gathered at his bedside to read the documents to him by the light of candles. Sir William signed them with a faltering hand, and then, having ordered some of his best sack to be brought, called for Henry Seymour and explained the day's events. Thomas Axe remembered the words his master spoke:

> Harry, I sent to thee to tell thee that I have beene now doeing what I have often done for thee, but would not tell thee till now that I thinke I shall not live longe. I have given thee all that I have and have obligded thee to take my name. Prithee Harry doe nothing unworthy of itt. Have a care of my honour.

Sir William Portman's faltering signature on his will dated 27 February 1690.
*Image: South West Heritage Trust*

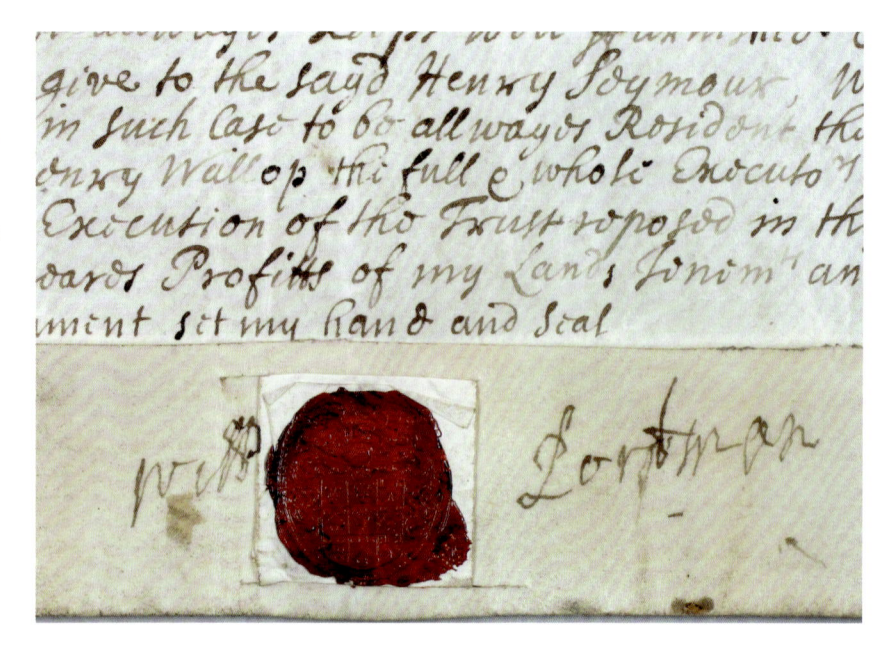

Henry Seymour then 'fell into a great passion' and wept, but Sir William merely said: 'What a fool you are. God be thanked, I am not afrayd to dye.' Sir William's servant, Henry Hooper, was with him on the last night of his life, 18 March 1690. Sir William asked for the bed curtains to be drawn, and some time afterwards turned himself and said, 'I shall die; Lord have mercy upon me.' The baronetcy acquired by his grandfather almost 80 years before died with him that night.[16]

The mourners were not detained long when Sir William was buried in the family vault ten days later. Perhaps he was too familiar with the 38-page eulogy preached for his uncle, Sir Hugh, in 1629 to wish his

Engraving of Sir William Portman (1644–1690), 6th baronet.
*Image: Somerset Archaeological and Natural History Society*

own funeral to be marked in a similar way. There would be no sermon, he insisted, 'seing it will hinder my friends from returning to their homes in good time'. Those friends, in any case, needed no reminder that the man they saw buried at Orchard had carried his family to new heights of wealth and influence, and had been important in some of the most significant events of his time.[17]

## Seymours and Berkeleys

Henry Seymour Portman (c. 1640–1728) was already fifty years old when he came into his unexpected inheritance. As the fifth son of his family he had lived under the shadow of his eldest brother, Sir Edward Seymour, and had achieved no more than a modest role for himself in the years before 1690. By 1662 he was serving as an ensign in the Guernsey garrison, in 1672–3 was a captain in the Duke of Buckingham's Regiment during the third Anglo-Dutch War, and in 1679 entered Parliament as the member for St Mawes in Cornwall. With few interruptions he remained an MP until 1715, latterly for Taunton, and was described as a Tory 'hearty for old England on its ancient basis'. He made little impression politically, being remembered instead as a 'jovial companion' who 'indulged his appetites', loved French wines and played backgammon. Almost the only preferment he seems to have achieved

Portrait of Henry Seymour Portman (c. 1640–1728), after Sir Godfrey Kneller, c. 1714. Sir William Portman, 6th baronet, chose his cousin Henry Seymour as his heir on condition that he took the surname Portman.
*Image: The Portman Estate*

Portrait of Meliora Fitch, second wife of Henry Seymour Portman, by Sir Godfrey Kneller, 1715.
*Image: Photography Courtesy of Sotheby's, Inc. ©2019*

was as Keeper of Hyde Park, a post he held from 1703 until his death, together with its salary of £200 a year.

In 1691, the year after he inherited, he consolidated his new wealth and status by marrying the heiress Penelope Haslewood, sister-in-law of Viscount Hatton. In 1714, after Penelope had died childless, he amazed the world by marrying Meliora Fitch, a girl reputedly only 14 years old and thus 60 years his junior. He had Sir Godfrey Kneller paint both their portraits, his own showing him somewhat absurdly as an elderly squire wearing armour, Meliora's depicting a demure young beauty dressed in red silk. Again there were no children of the marriage.[18]

Though Henry did not entirely abandon Orchard Portman, it was not his favourite home. He spent time in Bath, was frequently at Bryanston and also had a house in Hyde Park. But perhaps he was most attached to the fine classical townhouse he built in about 1720 at Sherborne, nearly midway between his principal seats in Somerset and Dorset. Sherborne House, with West Coker Manor, is the most complete surviving mansion of the Portman family built before the nineteenth century and is made memorable by the frescoes Henry Portman commissioned from Sir James Thornhill. They fill the staircase hall with scenes from the myth of Meleager, Diana and the Calydonian hunt, and suggest that Henry's tastes extended to classical literature. It was at Sherborne that Henry died on 23 February 1728, aged 88. He was brought back to Orchard one final time and on 15 March became the last head of Portman family to be buried in the family vault there.[19]

The will he drew up three years before he died reflects the man. The picture of his benefactor Sir William Portman, set with jewels and diamonds, was to go to Henry's niece Anne Berkeley (it may be the

*Frescoes in the staircase hall at Sherborne House, Dorset, painted for Henry Seymour Portman by Sir James Thornhill. They show scenes from the myth of Meleager, Diana and the Calydonian hunt.*
*Image: Sherborne House Trust*

miniature, without jewels, now in the Victoria and Albert Museum). There were generous benefactions to other friends and relations, including a snuff box set with diamonds for his godson Mr Courtenay, and another for Earl Poulett of Hinton St George. He was notably generous to many named servants, among them John Elliott 'my day labourer and workman' to whom he gave ten pounds. To his 'deare and well beloved wife' Meliora he left £10,000, his best chariot and a pair of his best coach horses. But he almost immediately repented of giving her his jewels and the 'greate pearle necklace' she usually wore. He revoked that bequest and instead left her the diamond earrings which, he explained, 'cost me neare twelve hundred pounds.' The monument that he asked should be set up near his grave was evidently never built.[20]

Henry's death without children meant that the provisions of Sir William Portman's settlement of 1690 again took effect. The new heir was William Berkeley (d. 1737) of Pylle in Somerset, grandson of

Sash and badge of a Knight of the Bath, *c.* 1550, reputedly worn by Sir Maurice Berkeley of Bruton (*c.* 1506–1581), Treasurer of the Household of Elizabeth I and ancestor of Edward Berkeley of Pylle, the grandfather of William Berkeley, later Portman (d. 1737).
*Image: The Portman Estate*

Philippa Speke and husband of Anne Seymour. He and his wife thus united two strands of the Portman family, both tracing descent from the first Portman baronet, Sir John, who had died over a century earlier. But Berkeley ancestry must have seemed even more important to the new head of the family. The Berkeleys had been prominent in the history of England since the Middle Ages, and not until 1736, eight years after inheriting, did William Berkeley at last obtain an Act of Parliament to change his name to Portman. He died the following year and was buried at Pylle.[21]

His son, by contrast, fully embraced his Portman destiny. Henry William Portman I (*c.* 1709–1761) at last established Bryanston as the family's principal home and lived there, it was said, 'in great affluence and hospitality' while at the same time observing 'the strictest rules of economy'. He was returned as MP for Taunton in 1734, then for Somerset in 1741, and before the Jacobite Rebellion in 1745 was described, perhaps fancifully, as one of the Young Pretender's most considerable supporters in England. Lord Egmont merely thought him 'a very odd man' though

The Manor House at Pylle, Somerset, home of William Berkeley (d. 1737), heir of Henry Seymour Portman. He took the surname Portman in 1736, eight years after inheriting.
*Image: Tom Mayberry*

a good Tory. Others remembered him as charitable to the poor as well as 'a gentleman of strict honour and integrity, punctual to his word and unbiased in his favours.'[22]

In 1734 he married Ann Fitch, who was the daughter of William Fitch of High Hall, Dorset, and the sister of Meliora. Ann has survived for us in Gainsborough's vast and magnificent portrait called 'The White Lady'. It was probably painted in about 1764, when she was already a widow, and is perhaps the greatest of all the treasures still in family possession.[23]

## Bryanston

Henry William Portman I died of gout in 1761 aged 52 and was succeeded by his only child Henry William Portman II (1738–1796).

According to the *London Evening Post* his birth in 1738 had been greeted with great joy, 'there having been no son born in the Portman family for many years before'.[24] He married Ann Wyndham in 1766, and was evidently a person of great vision and ability. He was destined to be the head of the family who began development of the London estate and also left an enduring mark at Bryanston.

The mansion lay a mile west of the Dorset town of Blandford Forum and had many similarities to the family's ancestral seat in Somerset. When the Portmans took possession, Bryanston had been held by the Rogers family since the early fifteenth century and like Orchard Portman had probably grown to incorporate a rambling mixture of medieval, Elizabethan and seventeenth-century elements. An incomplete inventory of 1690 records the great hall, the parlour, the dining room and the oriel, together with a 'closset or study' for Sir William Portman and other rooms for family members and close retainers. When Leonard Knyff depicted the house in a painting of about 1705 it consisted of a six-gabled Tudor mansion facing east towards the River Stour, flanked on its right-hand side by a later two-storeyed wing of classical design. Overshadowing all was what seems to have been a tall brick-built range in the Wren style. This new building was presumably commissioned by Sir William or by Henry Seymour Portman and was on a remarkably grand scale.[25]

The landscape surrounding the Tudor mansion skilfully combined the practical and the Arcadian. A map of 1659 shows the church and bowling green close at hand, and at a little distance the pound, the dove house and the home farm. Knyff's painting includes the tree-lined approach to Bryanston over the Blandford meadows and the two ornamental bridges which crossed the divided course of the River Stour. Just east of the mansion there was a large fountain, and to the south formal garden parterres reached up to the long wooded ridge called the Cliff.[26]

This was recognisably the place visited by the historian Edward Gibbon in May 1762 when he left a brief but vivid description of the estate and its owner, Henry William II:

> As to him, his good qualities, good nature, generosity and honor are his own, his faults, ignorance, and quickness of temper belong to his education, which was that of a spoilt child heir to six thousand a year. It is only to be feared that his love of fox hunting, hatred to London, and constant court of dependant persons, may in time reduce him to the contemptible character of a meer country squire. His place (on which and the House his father

laid out £25000) is delightfull. His cliff is the side of a hill about a mile long laid out with great taste, cut into a thousand walks, planted with great variety, and a river running at the bottom. The house is large and well fitted up, but inconvenient and ill-furnished. The prospects beautifull but confined.[27]

Portrait of Ann Portman (née Fitch), wife of Henry William Portman I, by Thomas Gainsborough, *c.* 1764. The portrait is known as 'The White Lady'.
*Image: The Portman Estate*

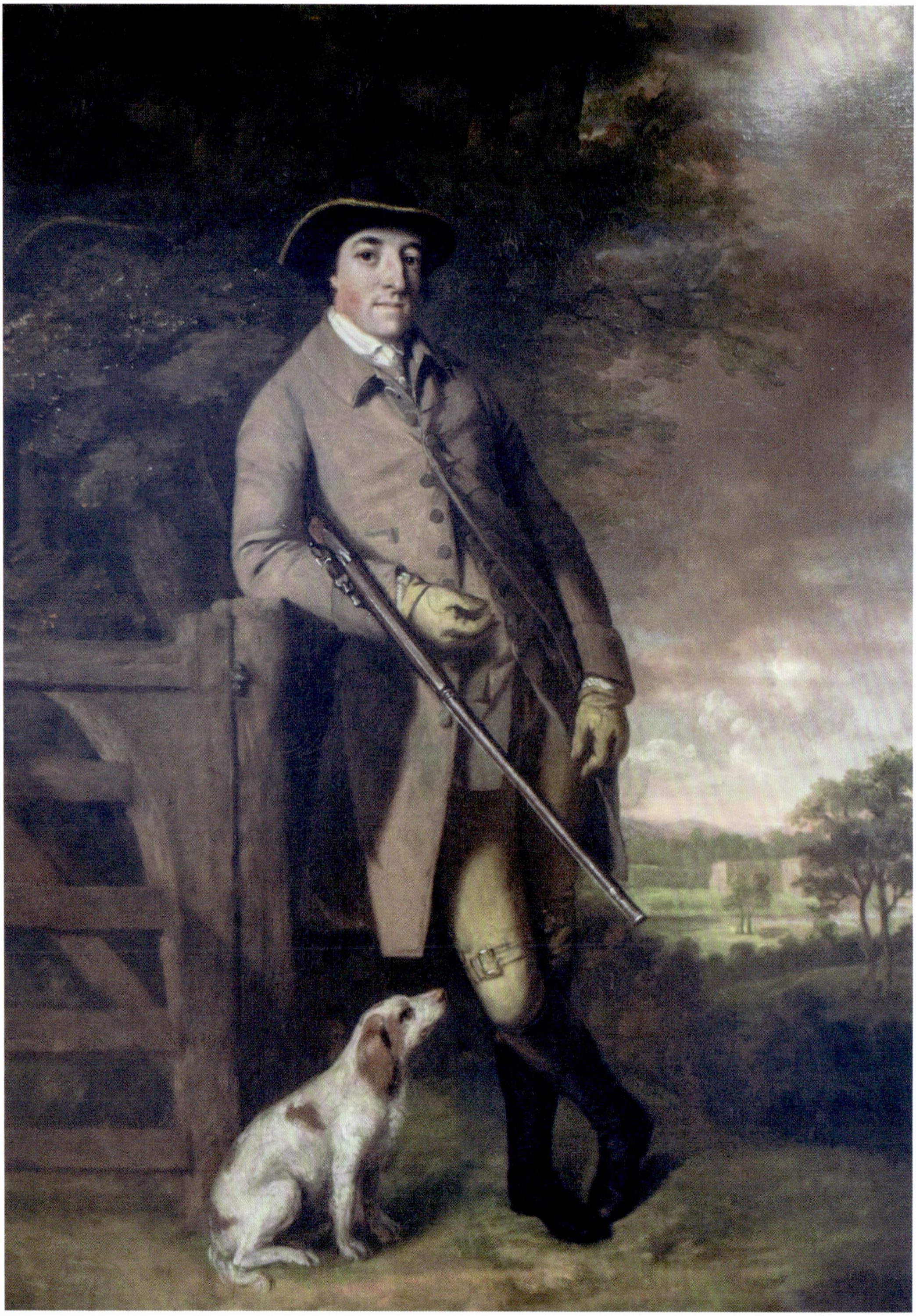

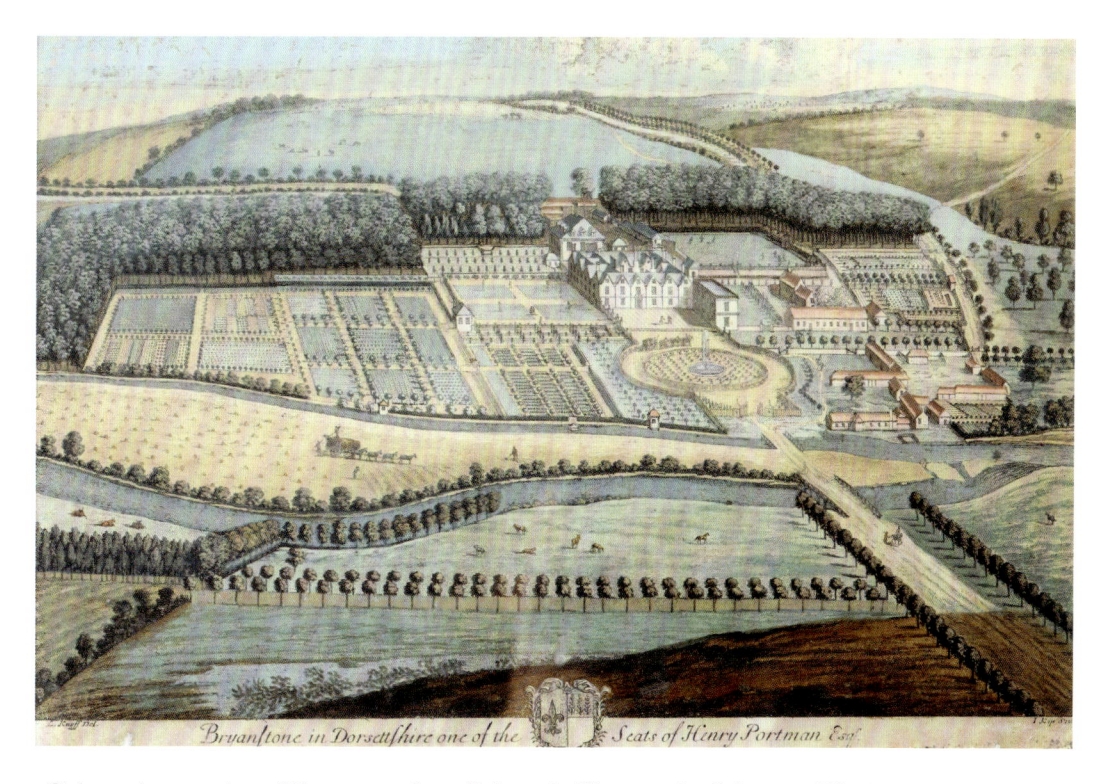

Coloured engraving of Bryanston from Britannia Illustrata by Johannes Kip, 1707/8, after a painting by Leonard Knyff.
*Image: Sabera Bham*

To achieve the seclusion he so desired, Henry William II spent many years seeking to divert the public rights of way which passed close to the mansion. In 1782 he succeeded, where his father had failed, in closing the horse and foot ways across the Blandford meadows. But not until 1794–5 was the road from Bryanston to Durweston, which passed immediately west of the house, finally closed. It survives today as the private entrance drive to the estate.[28]

The family now seldom visited Orchard Portman and, after greatly reducing the house in size in about 1786, they demolished it completely in about 1844.[29] Although Bryanston had become so much more a focus of Portman loyalty and investment it too was treated ruthlessly. In the

Portrait of Henry William Portman II (1738–1796) with James Wyatt's Bryanston House in the background.
*Image: The Portman Estate*

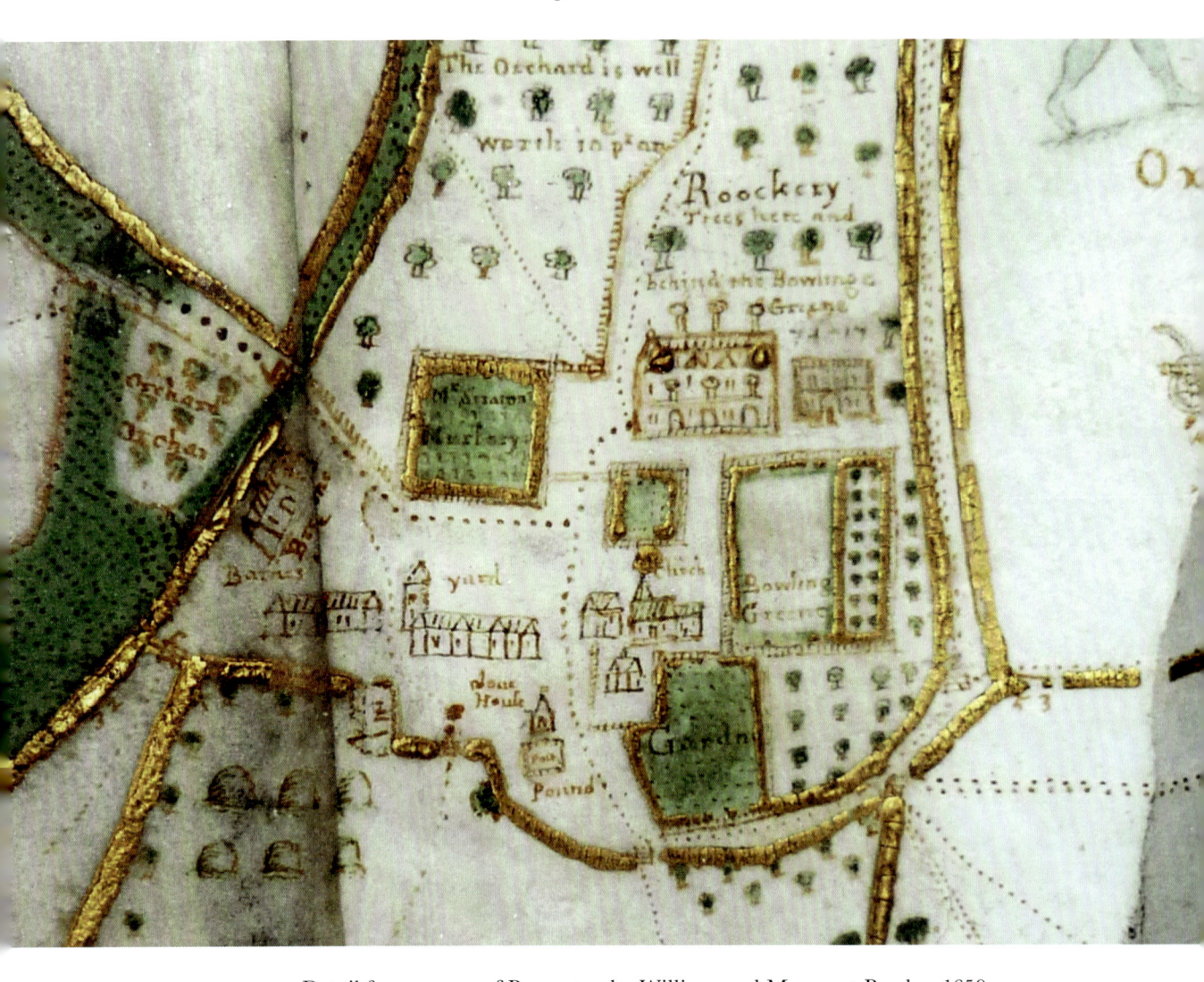

Detail from a map of Bryanston by William and Margaret Bowles, 1659.
*Image: The Portman Estate*

same years that Henry William II was beginning development of the London estate he also decided on a new start in Dorset. The Tudor Bryanston and its many additions were entirely swept away and on their site the fashionable architect James Wyatt was commissioned to build a fine new freestone mansion. It was ready for occupation in 1778.

Wyatt had spent six years in Italy acquiring his deep knowledge of classical forms and his mastery of spatial planning. The new Bryanston was typical of his early country house commissions. It was built on an almost square plan in a restrained classical style, with two main storeys and an attic. The entrance front was 112 feet wide and had a shallow three-bay portico with engaged Corinthian columns and a pediment rising above the line of the parapet.

The sober dignity of the exterior was complemented by the assured handling of the interior spaces. They were said to be 'finished in an elegant style, and admired for their proportions as well as their decorations.' The central feature was a dramatic full-height staircase hall, octagonal in plan, which was surrounded at first-floor level by a balcony. To the right of the entrance hall was the dining room and on

Engraving of the Wyatt mansion at Bryanston Dorset after J.P. Neale 1818.
*Image: Tom Mayberry*

the left the drawing room, leading to the music room and library. The 'very spacious and convenient' kitchen and servants' hall lay behind the main range of the house and were linked to it by a passage way. The group of buildings on the site was completed by the brewhouse, the stables and the Portman chapel of 1745.[30]

The work of transformation in these years was not limited to the rebuilding of the mansion. The formal gardens were replaced by an expansive landscaped park; the bridges across the Stour that linked Bryanston to the Blandford meadows were removed; and to emphasise the separation of this privileged domain from the busy life of Blandford, a classical gateway with Doric columns and flanking lodges was built at the southern entrance to the estate.[31]

By the 1780s the Arcadia of Bryanston was for the moment complete, but the new challenges and opportunities represented by London were now insistent. They would soon reshape the whole future of the Portman family.

James Wyatt's classical gateway at the southern entrance to Bryanston. It dates from about 1778.
*Image: Tom Mayberry*

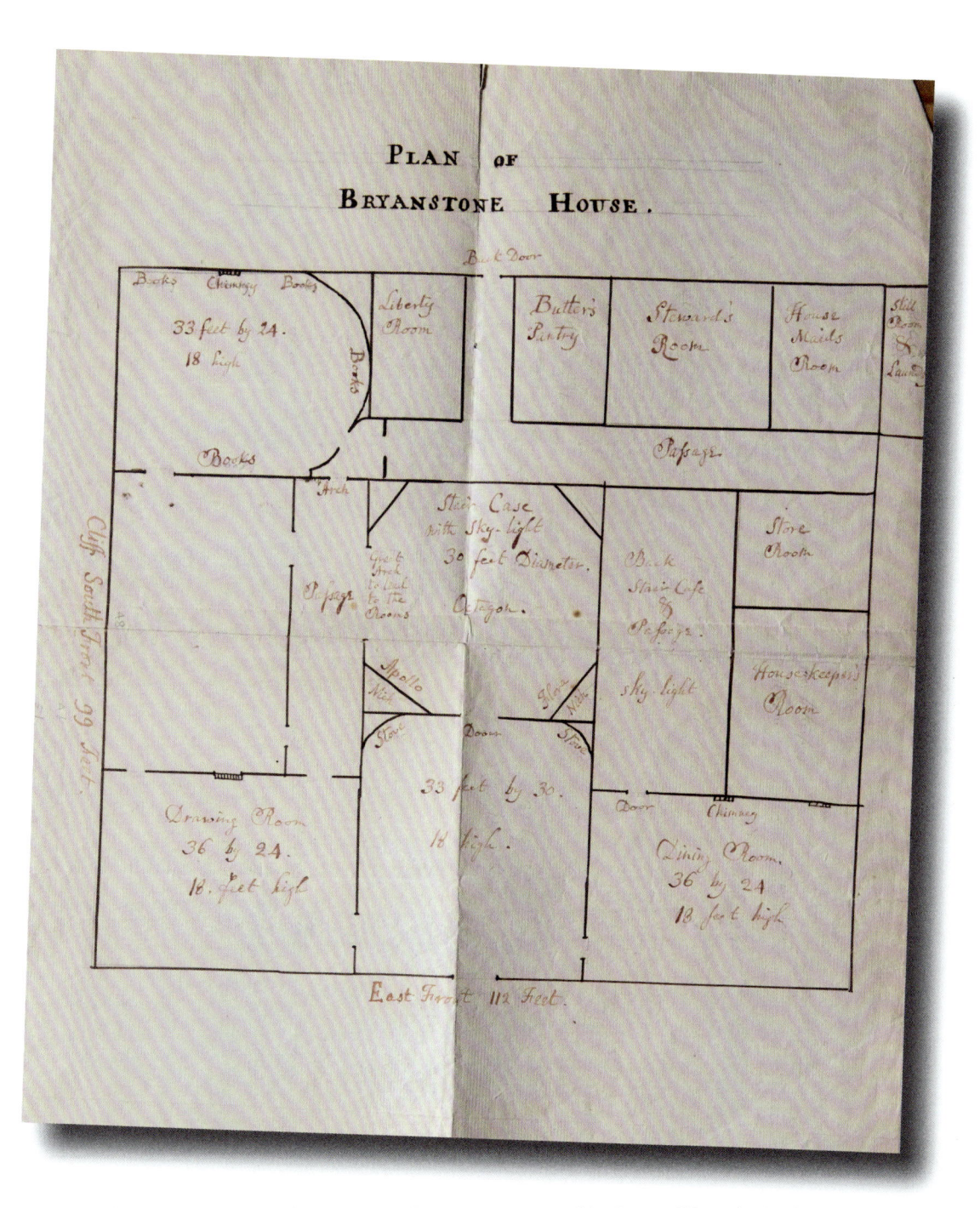

Ground floor plan of Bryanston House as completed by James Wyatt in 1778.
*Image: The Portman Estate*

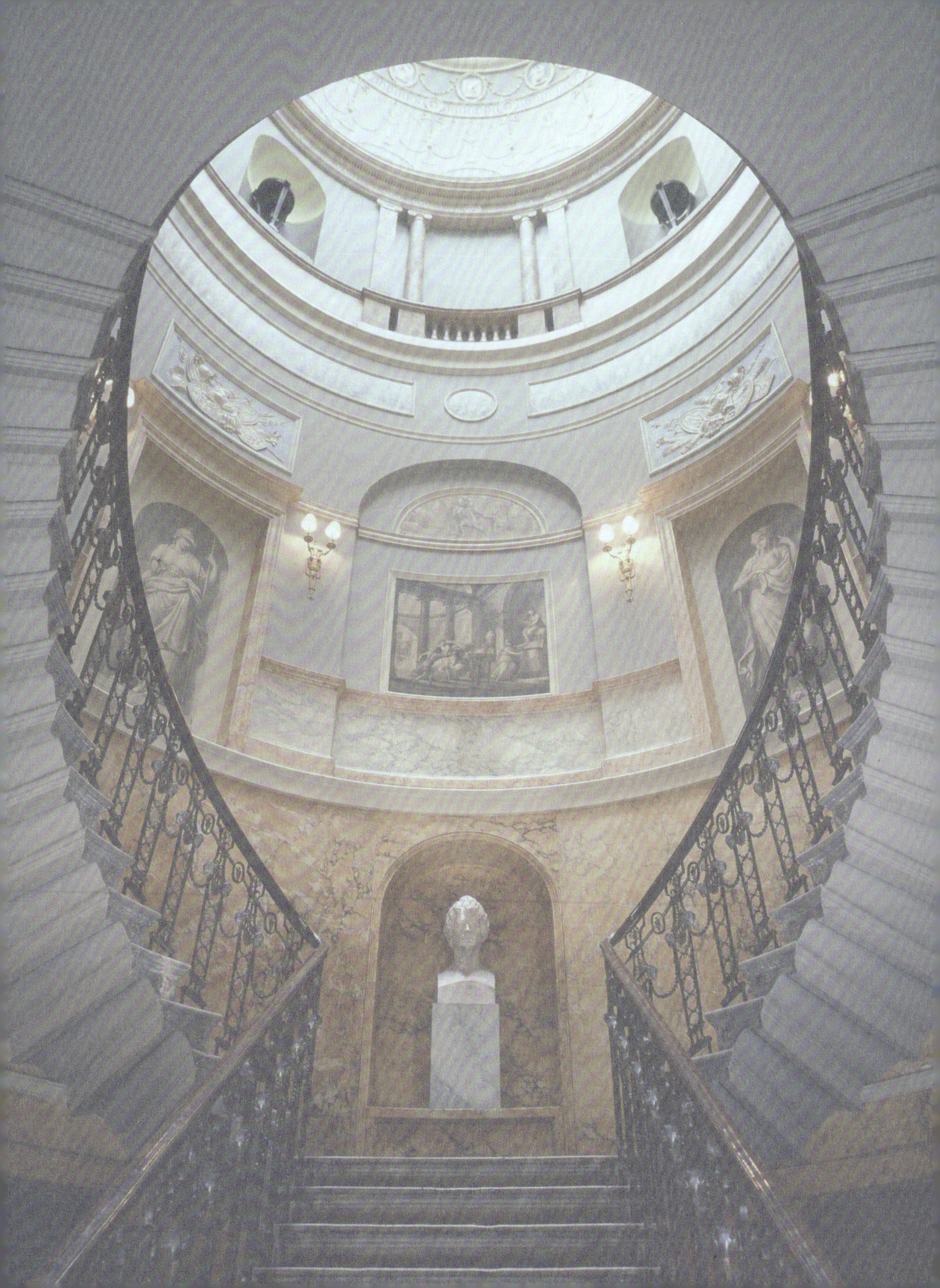

CHAPTER 3

# The Birth of the London Estate, 1755–1823

## *Marylebone Fields*

Portman ownership of the London estate long pre-dated the beginning of development there in the eighteenth century. It was acquired by the family in 1532 (making it London's oldest private estate) and fits like a jigsaw piece into a corner of Marylebone. Its curious shape reflects a history reaching back as far back as Domesday Book in 1086 when Marylebone was made up of the two manors of Tyburn and Lilestone, lying east and west of the Tyburn stream.[1]

Tyburn village grew up near the southern end of Marylebone Lane, where the Tyburn stream crossed Oxford Street, close to today's Bond Street. A dip in the road both there and in Wigmore Street marks the course of the stream as it flowed south on its way from Hampstead Heath. A parish church was built on the north side of Oxford Street in about 1200, but it was abandoned two hundred years later and a new church was built near Tyburn manor house, half a mile to the north.

By 1500 Thomas Hobson, an auditor of the Exchequer, was tenant of lands in the manor of Lilestone and also lord of the manor of Tyburn. He died in 1511 and control of the estate passed to John Blenerhasset, another senior official. On 1 July the following year the Prior of the Hospital of St John of Jerusalem, Clerkenwell, granted Blenerhasset and his wife Joan a 50-year lease of 11 fields in the manor of Lilestone, land

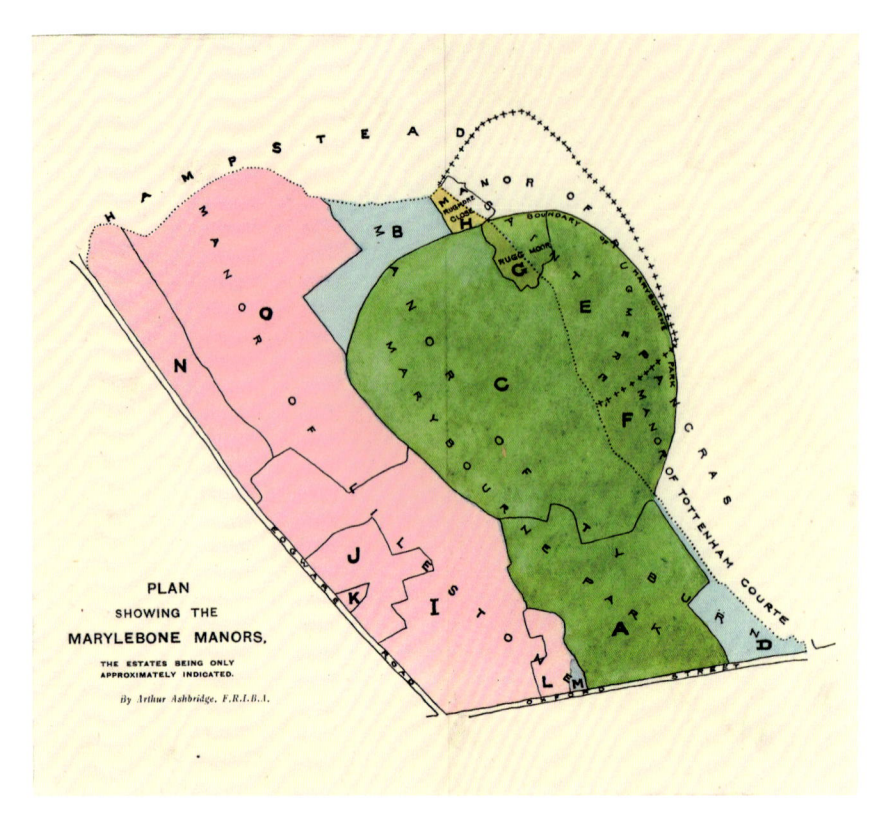

A plan showing Marylebone's manors and private estates. The letter 'I' indicates the Portman London estate.
*Image: © Westminster City Archives*

formerly held by Hobson. When John Blenerhasset died in 1532, William Portman, later the Lord Chief Justice, made his crucial investment, taking an assignment of the remaining 30-year term of the lease. The original lease of 1512 and the assignment to William Portman have both survived. So too have the Letters Patent of 1554 which granted Sir William, as he had by then become, the freehold of the estate.

In the leases of 1512 and 1532 the same 11 fields are listed by name as 'Great Gibbet Field, Little Gibbet Field, Hawkefield, Tasilcroft, le Beeche, Stanescroft, Royescroft, the Twenty Acres, Furcroft and two other closes or pastures called Shepecotehawe'. The gibbet is, of course, Tyburn gallows, a sinister if accepted feature of London life, which since the end of the twelfth century had stood at what is now the junction of Oxford Street and the Edgware Road, still the south-western corner of the estate.

## The Birth of the London Estate, 1755–1823

Assignment to Sir William Portman of a lease of 11 fields in the manor of Lilestone, 1532. This transaction was crucial in the history of the family and brought them their London estate.
*Image: The Portman Estate*

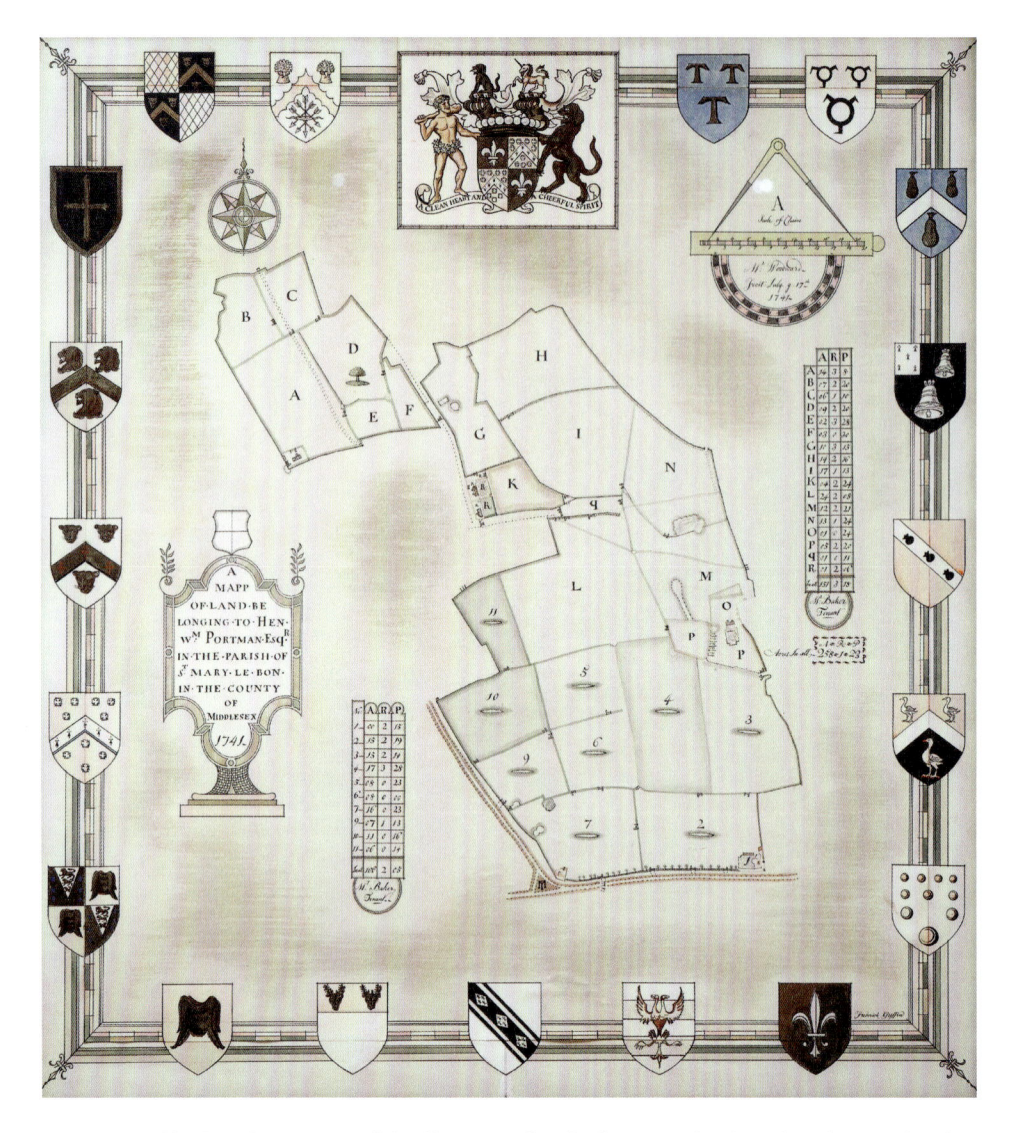

The London estate of the Portman family in 1741. At that date it contained 258 acres. On the left, at the junction of Oxford Street and Edgware Road, are the Tyburn gallows.
*Image: The Portman Estate*

By the time William Portman took possession of these lands in 1532, Marylebone's days as a remote village community were coming to an end. Shortly afterwards the Dissolution of the Monasteries plunged England into turmoil. The two manors of Tyburn and Lilestone reverted to the Crown and Henry VIII created Marylebone Park, a new royal hunting ground within easy reach of Whitehall Palace. It is a tribute to Sir William's skills that in spite of the turbulent events of the next twenty years he managed to keep hold of his property. The Letters Patent of 1554 excluded the land which was taken from his 11 fields to form Marylebone Park, but he was still left with a considerable estate, recorded in 1741 as containing 258 acres.[2] Why did he make this investment? The story goes that it was to provide goat's or ass's milk for an ailing member of the family, possibly his wife Elizabeth Gilbert. As it happens, 1532 was an important year for him, for this was when he achieved the distinction of being elected a Reader at the Middle Temple. Perhaps advancement in his career was one of the reasons for his decision to acquire Blenerhasset's lease.

For two hundred years the Marylebone fields remained farmland, though some accounts from around 1660 imply that the London estate was even then producing an annual rental of over £500, far more than any of the family's other properties.[3] That the London estate continued to be so valuable is confirmed in a series of accounts for 1737–1764.[4] Over this period of 27 years the average annual income from all the family's estates – 37 are listed – was around £8,500. To this sum the farmland at Marylebone contributed £900 a year, or 10.6% of the total. With this level of regular income being produced by the London estate it is not surprising that Henry William Portman I felt no immediate need to embark on a building programme.

## *Development Begins*

Almost no records have survived to tell us how development of the London estate was planned. The heart of the estate, around Portman Square, was built during the forty-year period from the end of the Seven Years' War in 1763, in what Sir John Summerson has called the 'golden age' of Georgian architecture. The estate was an immediate major addition to London's west end, and Portman Square itself, completed in about 1784, quickly achieved the sort of fashionable reputation that most developers could only dream of. Mrs Montagu, perhaps the square's most famous resident before Anthony Blunt, called it 'the Montpelier of England' and said that she had 'never enjoyed such health as since she came to live in it'.

The turning-point had been reached in 1755. On 20 September that year a lease of the entire estate was granted by Henry William Portman I to William Baker, a gentleman farmer from Shropshire, but by 1741

56     *From Somerset to Portman Square*

a major Portman tenant in London. The lease of 1755 described the estate as consisting of two farms. One was at Lisson Green and was occupied by William Baker himself. The other was based halfway along Oxford Street, next to the White Hart public house, which stood on the site where, 150 years later, Harry Gordon Selfridge would build his department store. The lease to Baker was of special significance because for the first time it permitted building development to take place, subject to individual building leases granted by the estate. Orchard Street and Portman Street were the first two streets to be built, taking their names from the original family home in Somerset. Individual properties were also built between them along the north side of Oxford Street. Having started at the south-east corner of the estate, development spread north and west. John Rocque's London map of 1761 shows how quickly the

An extract from John Rocque's map of London, 1769. Marylebone was then on the very edge of London, with fields to the north and west.
*Image: London Metropolitan Archive*

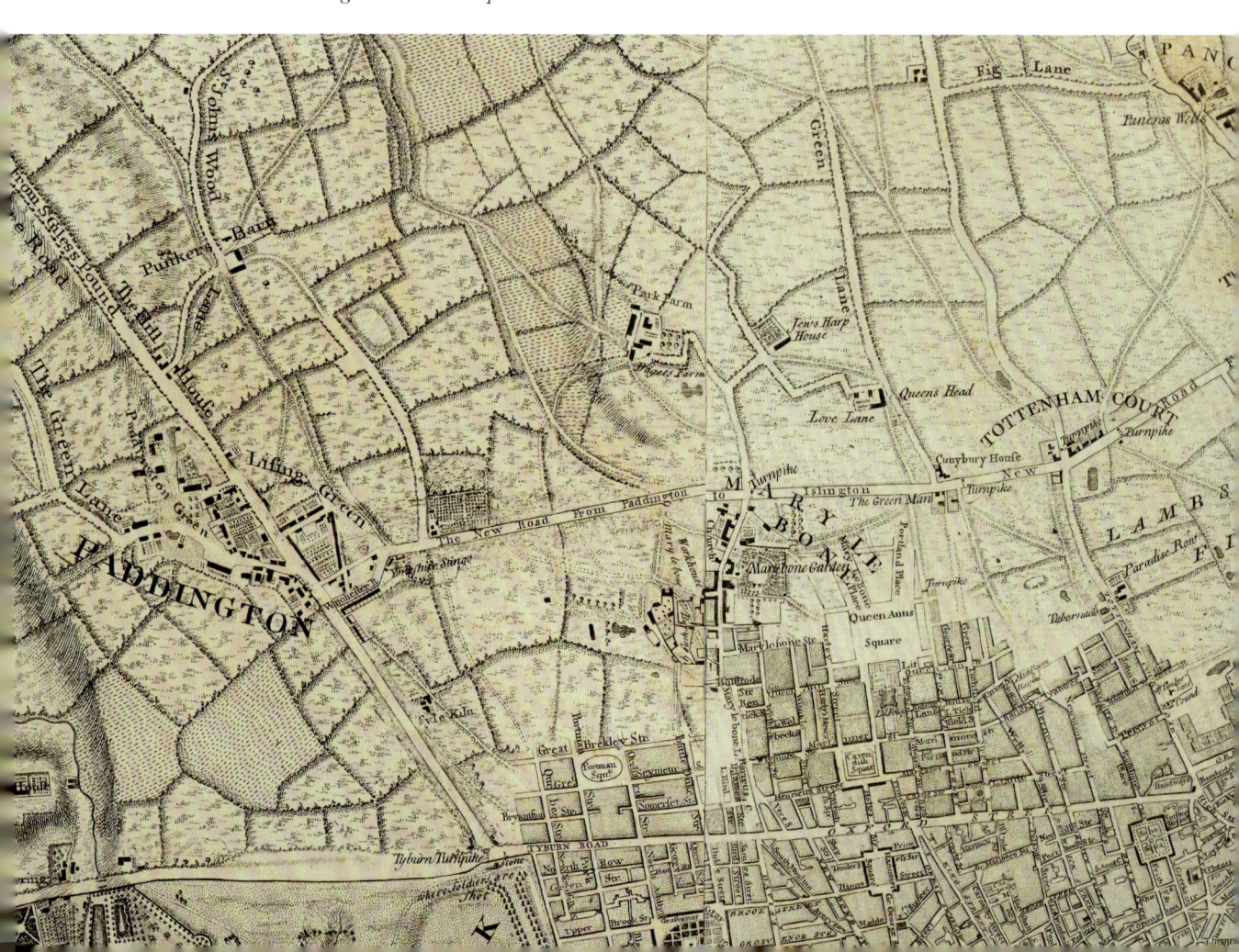

streets were built, all of them named after the Portman family or their West Country homes. The notable exception was Quebec Street, for which building leases were being granted in 1759, the year of General Wolfe's victory and death at the Battle of Quebec.

A prominent feature shown on Rocque's map is the 'New Road from Paddington to Islington'. It provided a major east–west route on the northern side of the estate and originally comprised the modern Marylebone Road, Euston Road and Pentonville Road. An Act of Parliament, passed in May 1756, was required before the road could be built and followed a petition presented six months earlier by a group of nine local landowners, including Henry William Portman I. The New Road has been called the world's first bypass and discussions about it had begun some years earlier – it is shown on one of John Rocque's maps dated 1754.[5] The prospect of such an important route crossing his estate was probably a key factor in prompting Henry William Portman to grant the lease to William Baker in 1755, and to allow development to begin. He must surely have recognised that the New Road could make his own undeveloped estate a highly desirable residential area. As the petition to Parliament said, the road would help 'persons of quality', such as lived in the 'great squares' and elegant streets of neighbouring estates, to 'come into the city without being jolted three miles over the stones or perhaps detained three hours by a stop in some narrow street.'

By the time the New Road was being marked out across the fields, Parliament realised that it would also provide a much faster route for the army if it needed to march round London from the north in order to defend the country. This was a important consideration at a time when the war with France was spreading from America to Europe, and was one reason for the road's great width – 60 feet in the case of the Marylebone section. It is striking as well that instead of a chapel or a market, such as were often built at an early stage on private estates, one of the very first buildings to be erected behind Oxford Street was a large Riding House, which by June 1757 was being used as stables by His Majesty's First Troop of Life Guards.[6] The very limited sources for this period of the estate's history do not record why the decision to build the stables was made, though we do know that they were converted into the Portman Foot Barracks during the mid-1790s. A number of new barracks were being built in central London at about the same period in response to the concerns raised by the Gordon Riots as well as by the threat from France. The barracks remained in use until 1858.

## The Leasehold System

By the middle of the eighteenth century private estates were already very much part of the London scene. The Earl of Bedford's Covent Garden estate had been developed under the direction of Inigo Jones as early as the 1630s, and was followed thirty years later by the Earl of Southampton's development of Bloomsbury. Then, in about 1715, development started on the Grosvenor and the Harley (or Portland) estates, immediately to the south and east of Portman territory. In each case a main square was created as the heart of the new development, just as would happen when in 1764 building leases were issued for the first houses in Portman Square.

Under the leasehold system as it operated on these estates, the landowner drew up the outline development plans. In the case of the development plans for Marylebone, it was the new tenant, William Baker, who undertook this work, assisted by James Buck, the surveyor who made the early plans of the Portman estate, his son George, who later became the agent to the estate, and one or two others. The estate

Coloured engraving by Rudolph Ackermann showing the north side of Portman Square, 1813. By this date Portman Square was one of the most fashionable addresses in London.
*Image: © The Trustees of the British Museum*

The music room of Home House, 20 Portman Square, in 1931 when Samuel Courtauld and his wife were living there. *Image: Conway Library, The Courtauld Institute of Art, London*

worked with a large number of builders, first entering into a detailed building agreement for each individual plot, or sometimes a group of plots. When the carcase of a building was complete a lease would be granted to the builder, often for 99 years at a low or even a peppercorn rent, and once the building was complete the builder would assign the lease to the first occupier. It was the occupier and his successors who then became responsible for paying the full annual ground rent. (The date of every building lease, together with the name of the builder, is recorded in the two 'Red Books' still preserved in the estate archives.)

The staircase and circular stairwell at Home House, 20 Portman Square. This spectacular space is top-lit by a domed skylight.
*Image: The Portman Estate*

This elaborate system was well-tried and gave the Portmans a very high level of control over the development of the estate and its subsequent management.[7]

## Portman Square

Unlike Bedford Square, developed between 1775 and 1783 to a unified design, Portman Square was from the first intended as a series of ambitious separate houses built to individual commissions. In the language of the London Building Act of 1774, which defined four 'rates' or classes of dwelling, Portman Square contained only 'First Rate' houses, with the largest floor areas and highest ground rents.

By 1772, the east, west and south sides of the square had been completed and were at once occupied by wealthy and aristocratic tenants. Most of the building leases were issued to the brothers Abraham and Samuel Adams. They were not related to the more famous Adam brothers, but were nevertheless highly competent local builders who were responsible for much other construction on the estate.

Most of the north side of the square was built under the supervision of the architect James Wyatt, whose spectacular Pantheon building had been opened in Oxford Street in 1772. He designed 20 Portman Square for Elizabeth, Countess of Home, but by the end of 1774 she had dismissed him and appointed Robert Adam to complete the work. The result was a dazzling example of Adam's decorative skills and what is accepted as his finest surviving London house. It is also one of only three original houses that remain in the square.

It is not known what caused the falling out between Wyatt and the Countess of Home. Wyatt was certainly erratic and slow to complete the north side of the square, but it may have been the competing demands of another commission which led to his dismissal. For, as has already been recorded, it was at this very time that Henry William Portman II decided to rebuild the family mansion at Bryanston. The Countess of Home, like other local inhabitants, was a larger than life character.[8] An heiress to property in the West Indies, including sugar plantations founded on slavery, she was known as the 'Queen of Hell' because of her extravagant parties and the company she kept. But even she was eclipsed as a hostess by Mrs Elizabeth Montagu, her neighbour at 22 Portman Square (Montagu House).

This magnificent mansion, standing in its own grounds on the north-west corner of the square, was designed for Mrs Montagu by James 'Athenian' Stuart and completed in 1781. Later it became the Portman family's London home but was badly damaged in the Second World War and demolished as a result. The Portman Hotel now occupies part of the site. When Mrs Montagu moved there from Mayfair, she was a wealthy widow already established as London's leading literary hostess and known, by contrast with the Countess of Home, as the 'Queen of the Bluestockings'. She was also famous for entertaining London's chimney sweeps to a dinner of roast beef and plum pudding every May Day 'so that they might enjoy *one* happy day in the year'. The popular explanation for her generosity was the story that a young member of the Montagu family had been kidnapped and made to work as a climbing boy. What is certain is that David Porter, the builder largely responsible for Montagu Square, had himself been a chimney sweep when young and did much, with Mrs Montagu's support, to reform their conditions.

Only a short distance from the square, 28 Orchard Street was also a centre for fashionable society. It was there that the playwright Richard Brinsley Sheridan and his beautiful wife, the soprano Elizabeth Linley, first settled after their marriage in 1773, and there that Sheridan wrote his great comedy, *The Rivals*. Jane Austen may have visited her brother Henry at 24 Upper Berkeley Street, where he lived from 1801 to 1804, and nearby were the artists Richard Cosway, the miniaturist, and George Stubbs. From 1764 to 1806 Stubbs lived at 24 Somerset Street. His remarkable painting 'The Royal Tiger' was acquired by the Portmans in 1807 and remained in their ownership until 1995.

## *The Estate Spreads North*

William Baker died in 1774, aged 59, and for the next three years trustees acted for his son, Peter William Baker, who was a minor. Maps and plans of the estate at this period help us to trace its rapid expansion northward. A plan of 1780 includes the newly-completed Manchester Square as well as the line of the street that would be named in William Baker's honour. The same plan shows the full extent of the estate north of the New Road, and clearly marks the as-yet unbuilt Lisson Grove. There were also new stables for the 2nd Troop of Life Guards. The stables were evidently financed, like much else on the estate, by the rich and eccentric John Elwes (1714–1789), who had a house in Portman Square. Some ideas at first went unrealised. A plan of 1777 shows a large market place near Manchester Square, but another fifty years would pass before the market was finally created much farther north.

By 1794, when the first edition of Richard Horwood's map of London appeared, Baker Street was almost complete, the River Tyburn had disappeared into a culvert, terraced houses with long front gardens lined the New Road, and the circus originally planned for Great Cumberland Place had instead become a crescent. The third edition of Horwood's

*The Birth of the London Estate, 1755–1823*

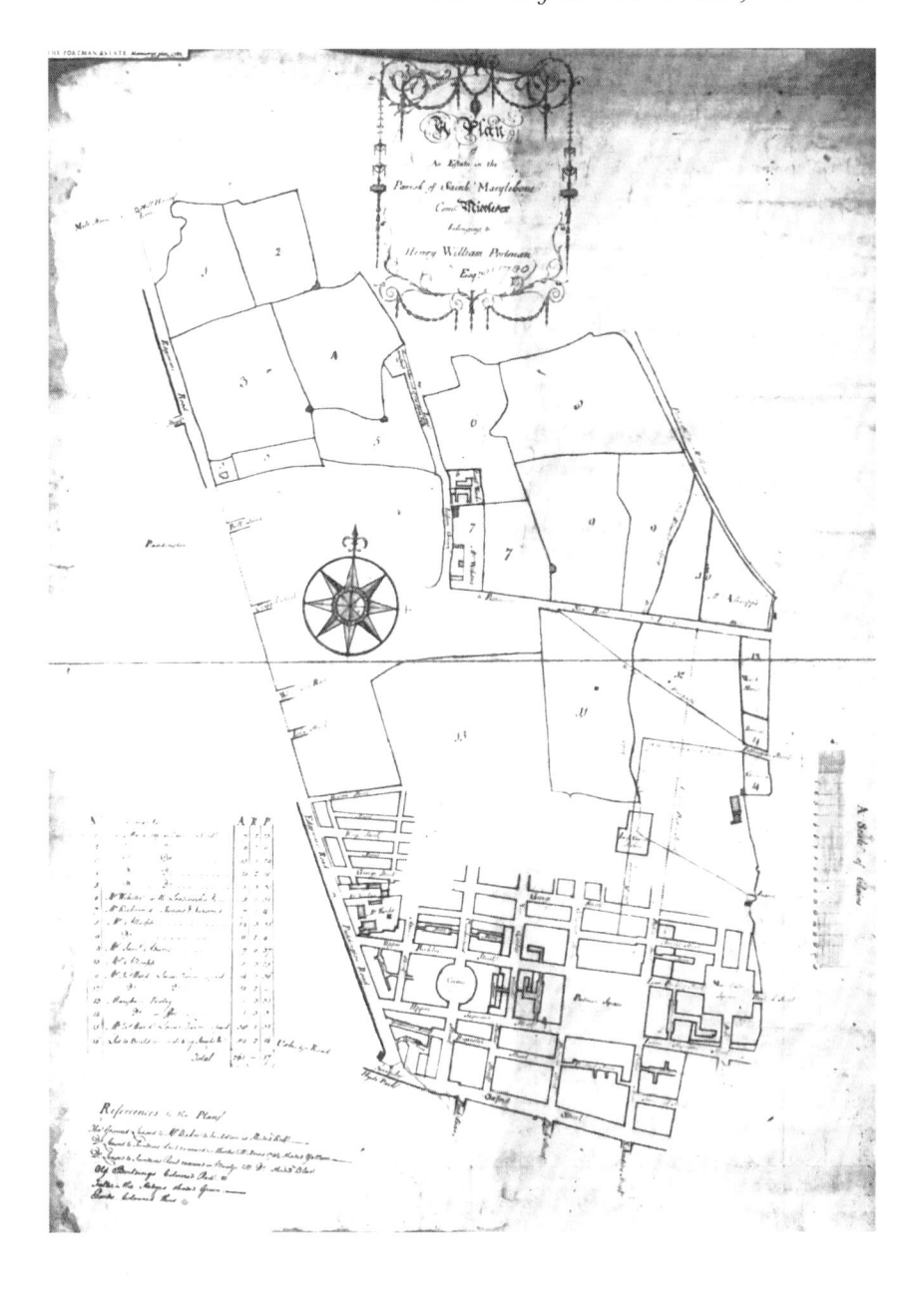

A plan of the estate in 1780.
*Image: Richard Bowden*

map in 1813 shows Montagu Square complete and Bryanston Square well under way. By the 1820s a series of three maps shows the entire area south of the New Road complete, with further development, including Dorset Square, beginning to the north of it.[9]

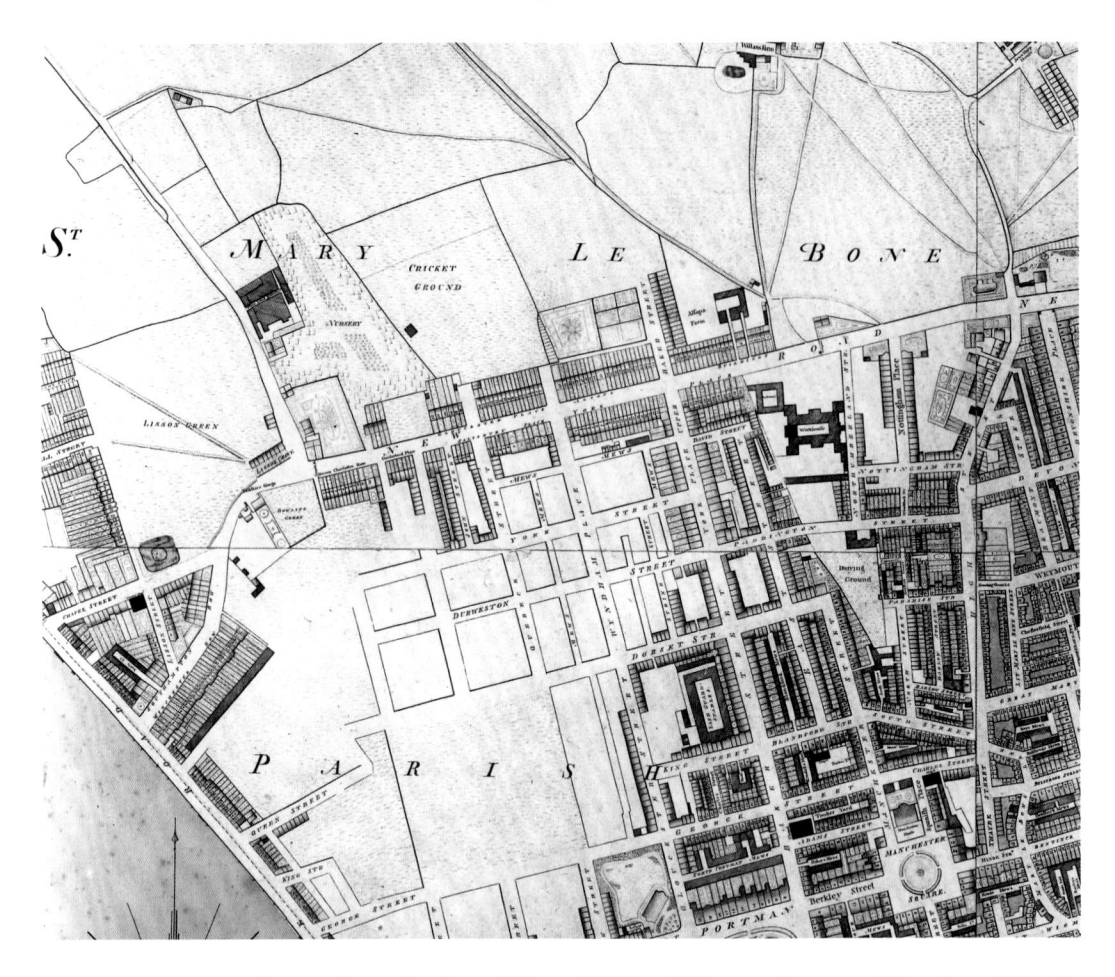

Extract from the first edition of Richard Horwood's map of London, 1794. It is the earliest printed map to show the estate in detail and provides evidence of its rapid expansion at that time.
*Image: The Portman Estate*

## Social Conditions

The wealthy residents of Portman Square depended on the servants and tradesmen who lived nearby in small insanitary courts and mews dwellings. Before 1800 a house in Portman Square might have a rateable value of up to £600 a year, but a house in one of these courts might be rated at as little as £10 and offered living conditions of the meanest kind. An example was Calmel Buildings, a small close next to Orchard Street, which was notorious as a colony for Irish immigrant labourers. Three or four families might live together in a single room, and in 1816 an official report also referred to over a hundred pigs being kept there. Gin drinking and crime were prevalent and until the 1820s no proper police force existed to keep the peace. According to visitors from abroad, such as Johann Wilhelm von Archenholz, prostitution also flourished, though it was probably always more common in the area further east, later known as Fitzrovia, than around Portman Square.[10]

At the same time there were increasing attempts to make London a more civilised place. In 1739 the capital's first lying-in hospital was founded in Jermyn Street, moving in 1763 to Old Quebec Street on the Portman estate. The bodies of a number of children, and even of one mother, were found buried at the back of the house in 1766. But the hospital survived the scandal, transferring first to 243 Oxford Street and then, in 1813, to a more permanent home at the top of Harcourt Street. Under the name of Queen Charlotte's Hospital, it stayed there

William Hogarth's engraving 'The Idle 'Prentice Executed at Tyburn', 1747.
Executions attracted crowds of up to 200,000 people.
*Image: © Westminster City Archives*

Coloured engraving by Rudolph Ackermann showing Tyburn Turnpike, 1813.
*Image: The Portman Estate*

until 1940 and was supported throughout by members of the Portman family. In 1814 the pharmacy Meacher, Higgins and Thomas opened at 105A Crawford Street where it still flourishes today.

Another long-overdue improvement took place in 1783 when, after 600 years, Tyburn ceased to be London's place of public execution, a role which was taken over by Newgate Prison. By 1813, when Rudolph Ackermann chose the ancient gallows site for one of the engravings in his *Repository of Arts*, it was associated with the toll house of the Marylebone Turnpike Trust, and the view along Oxford Street, rather than with the hangman's noose. Timber from the gallows is said to have been converted into stands for beer butts in the cellars of the Carpenter's Arms in Seymour Place.[11]

Among the most striking aspects of these early decades in the development of the estate are the enormous power exercised by its owner, his evident sense of responsibility and, usually, his good taste. He was creating something intended to last for generations and which in consequence needed to be planned, designed, built and managed to excellent standards. The Portman family's judgement was based partly on current fashions and ways of thinking, but could rely as well on centuries of experience in looking after the West Country estates, where many of the same principles had long been applied.

## Church Building

One immediate need in the early years of the London estate was for a new parish church. Marylebone's population increased rapidly during the eighteenth century and the little parish church at the top of the High Street soon became inadequate. The burial ground on the south side of Paddington Street, given by the Earl of Oxford in 1730, was also far too small. In 1772 Henry William Portman II offered a solution to both problems, suggesting that the centre of a new square he was then planning (later Manchester Square) should be the site for a church and that land on the north side of Paddington Street could serve as an additional burial ground. His only condition was that the new church should be built within seven years.[12]

The new burial ground quickly came into use, but the church was more problematic. Ground conditions at the Manchester Square site were not firm enough for a building on the intended scale and the trustees of the new church were thus obliged to pay Henry William Portman II the sum of £3,000 for breaking the conditions of his original grant of land. In 1774 a fine new building of another kind rose in the square. This was the town house of the Duke of Manchester, after whom the square was named, and who, remarkable as it may seem, was attracted to the location because if offered good duck shooting, close to the Tyburn stream. The square was largely complete by 1780.

The argument about the new church continued for another forty years, not least because Henry William Portman II and the Duke of Portland both wanted the church on their own estate. Because of the failure to agree, both estates built proprietary chapels instead, of which the Portman Estate had two. One was the Portman Chapel in Baker Street which was opened in 1779 and known from 1900 as St Paul's Church. The other was the Quebec Chapel of 1788 in Bryanston Street, which later became the Church of the Annunciation and was rebuilt in 1914. The Duke of Portland, for his part, built the Brunswick Chapel in Upper Berkeley Street in 1795. These chapels were not licensed for baptisms, marriages or burials and were effectively commercial undertakings where pews were rented to the wealthy who came to hear sermons and, of course, to be seen. Vaults beneath the chapels were a further convenient source of income and were often rented as wine-cellars.

Though Marylebone's two greatest landowners failed to agree on a site for the parish church, they did cooperate in other ways. In 1775, for example, they provided land for a new, much larger, workhouse on the south side of the New Road.

## More Squares

After the intensive development work of the 1770s and '80s there was a pause during the 1790s until work began on the larger squares. Montagu Square was created in the period 1804–12, Bryanston Square in 1811–21 and Dorset Square in 1812–26. There is no record of where the idea originated for building Montagu and Bryanston Squares. They are among the estate's most striking features, and although their layout was much criticised in the past, they are now greatly admired. (There used to be a 'cluster of small cottages' nearby called Apple Village.[13] One wonders whether this happy coincidence encouraged John Lennon to move to 34 Montagu Square in 1968.) It is likely that men such as Peter William Baker and George Buck, the agent, were responsible for the overall design of these two squares, no doubt with help from the Portman family. We know that David Porter was largely responsible for actually building Montagu Square, as well as Dorset Square and much else both north and south of the New Road.[14] He also built 68 Great Cumberland Place, a house overlooking Bryanston Square, as an office for George Buck. From here Buck would have been able to keep a close eye on the work in progress. The office of George Buck's successor, Thomas Wilson, at 12 Montagu Street, was again on a corner site giving good views of the developing estate.

From the beginning special trusts were set up by Act of Parliament to administer the gardens in the estate's squares. The system worked so well that the trusts still exist today. Trustees were empowered to raise a small rate from the residents of each square so that the gardens could be cared for and perennial problems such as damage by dogs and children, and illegally-held keys, could be dealt with. Only residents of the squares were allowed access to the gardens. General access is still limited but the gardens in Portman Square are now open to the public on certain days during the summer months.[15]

*View of Lisson Green looking east, c.1770.*
*Image: © Westminster City Archives*

## Local Administration

By 1800 St Marylebone had become the wealthiest parish in England and also one of the best run. The St Marylebone parish vestry – the equivalent of one of today's borough councils – was responsible through the Justices of the Peace and the Court of Petty Sessions for a mass of local matters. They included the relief of the poor, law and order, fire prevention, paving, cleaning and lighting the streets (including from around 1820 gas lighting) and dealing with water companies. The estate was kept fully in touch by individuals such as George Buck, who was himself actively involved as a vestryman for many years.[16] As the estate was privately owned, many local matters were jointly decided by the landowner and the relevant authority. Alehouse licences, for example, were granted by the magistrates, but the estate took the initial decision over where the public houses should be located. More than

200 years later a number of them are still flourishing. They include the Three Tuns in Portman Mews South, the Grazing Goat (formerly the Bricklayer's Arms) in New Quebec Street, and the Carpenter's Arms and the Portman Arms (formerly the Mason's Arms) both in Seymour Place. The Three Tuns dates from 1765 and is the oldest surviving public house on the estate, while the other three were part of the next phase of building, ten years later.

## French Émigrés

The 1790s were a time when the threat of French invasion dominated the thinking both of politicians and the public. Volunteer corps were formed all over the country, and the two sons of Henry William Portman II, Henry and Edward, both served in the Dorset Yeomanry. Marylebone had two volunteer units of its own. The first was formed in 1797 but disbanded four years later when there was a brief peace

The St Marylebone Volunteers on parade in Dorset Fields, 1797. In the background are some of the terraces that lined the New Road.
*Image: © Westminster City Archives*

Watercolour by T. Appleton of the French Chapel Royal, also known as the Chapel of the Annunciation, Little George Street, Marylebone, 1890.
*Image: © Westminster City Archives*

with France. The second lasted from 1802 to 1814 as the Royal York St Marylebone Volunteers, taking its name from the Duke of York who was Commander-in-Chief of the British Army and lived in Portman Square. There he could be conveniently close to his mistress, Mary Ann Clarke, who lived at 62 Gloucester Place. (He suffered a serious disgrace when she was later found to be selling army commissions.)

It was also in the 1790s that the Marylebone estate provided refuge for a large number of French Catholic émigrés who were fleeing from revolutionary Paris. The presence of the French ambassador at 20 Portman Square at this time was probably the main reason they chose Marylebone as a place to settle. The new arrivals were soon so numerous that they persuaded the estate, in an intensely anti-Catholic age, to allow them to build a chapel of their own. Known as the French Chapel Royal, it stood in Little George Street (later renamed Carton Street). Two future kings of France, Louis XVIII and Charles X, were married there, and many members of the French royal family lived nearby until they were able to return to France. The chapel itself remained in use as a Catholic place of worship until 1911 and was demolished only in 1969 when plans were being drawn up for this corner of the estate.[17]

## Beyond the New Road

North of the New Road the character of the estate changed. Near the site of William Baker's farm at Lisson Grove the composer Josef Haydn spent the summer of 1791 during his first London visit and Thomas Jenkins opened a nursery garden, which prospered for many years. Close by was the white lead manufactory shown on Horwood's map of 1793. But perhaps the most important feature on the map is Thomas Lord's cricket ground, where the Marylebone Cricket Club was founded in 1787. Lord was an ambitious Yorkshireman who had opened a wine shop two years earlier on the corner of Gloucester Place. His business flourished, and so did his cricket ground in 'Dorset Fields', which Lord, with characteristic business acumen, also let for other events including regimental parades and even in 1802 a balloon ascent.

Image from The Laws of Cricket as drawn up in 1788 at Thomas Lord's cricket ground, now Dorset Square.
*Image: © Westminster City Archives*

Engraving showing Monsieur André Garnerin's balloon ascent in 1802. It was intended as a peace gesture.
*Image: © The British Library Board*

The ascent took place during the peace with France and attracted a vast crowd, including the Prince Regent himself. The occasion was marred by the collapse of one of the stands which resulted in fatalities. It also rained, leading *The Times* to comment that 'in the mud several of the ladies lost their shoes before reaching their carriages'. It was, at least, a more successful celebration than had occurred shortly before in Portman Square itself. The French embassy, then on the south side of the square, laid on a lavish entertainment to celebrate the Treaty of Amiens, illuminating the front of the embassy with lamps forming the word 'Concord'. The crowd read this as 'Conquered' and furiously stormed the building. The ambassador at once rearranged the lamps to read 'Amitié' but the crowd, reading this as 'Enmity', attacked again. Only when the word 'Peace' appeared were they finally satisfied.

In 1811 Dorset Square was being planned and Thomas Lord was as a result forced to move his cricket ground. Almost at once he had to

'Coloured acquatint, after A. C. Pugin, showing illuminations at the French embassy, then on the south side of Portman Square, marking the short-lived peace with France, 1802.
*Image: London Metropolitan Archive*

move again, this time because of plans to build the Regent's Canal, a scheme in which the new head of the Portman family, Edward Berkeley Portman I, took a close and critical interest. The canal was to prove an important determining factor in the development of the whole area around Lisson Grove.

The Grand Junction Canal had reached Paddington Basin in 1801, and when the architect John Nash began to create Regent's Park in 1811 the idea was revived of constructing a canal link through the park to the Thames at Limehouse. When the scheme came before Parliament in 1812 it was vigorously opposed, including by Edward Berkeley Portman I, on the grounds of the disturbance and damage it would cause. He estimated the value of his estate at £8 million and said that if the canal was built along the proposed route 27,000 people would be adversely affected and he would be prevented from spending £200,000 in the area.[18] His views, though undoubtedly overstated, were influential and as a result the line of the canal was moved slightly north, avoiding Portman land. In addition a tunnel was built for it between Edgware Road and Lisson Grove.

Construction of the Regent's Canal was a huge task. On the first two editions of Peter Potter's Plan of St Marylebone, dating from 1821 and about 1824, the open area beside the Edgware Road is described as 'Portman Green, a space covered with Temporary Cottages and Gardens'.[19] This was where labourers working on the canal lived with their families. After the canal opened in 1820 Edward Berkeley Portman I leased the majority of that portion of the estate to James Thompson Parkinson, the architect largely responsible a few years earlier for the Bryanston Square development. But by now much of the area had been changed forever.

My dear Lady Fortescue

Having had the pleasure of being personally acquainted with you for some years, and having always had a great esteem for your whole Family, I should be delighted to appoint your one of My Ladies of the Bedchamber

CHAPTER 4

# Family Matters

*Disinheritance*

Having presided over the development of the estate for much of his adult life, Henry William Portman II died in 1796. He left two sons, Henry and Edward, but disinherited Henry as his heir in a will drawn up just after Henry's marriage to Lucy Dormer in May 1793.[1] The reasons are obscure, though there is some indication that the aging head of the family soon had second thoughts. It is recorded that Henry, who had been MP for Wells since 1790, resigned from Parliament in January 1796 after his father's death, having indeed become heir to the estate.[2] Other evidence suggests that Edward was by then actually managing it, an impression confirmed by the first surviving income tax return for the estate, dated 1799, which is in the name of Edward Berkeley Portman of Bryanston. The return records a total annual income of £14,200, of which £5,000 came from Marylebone.[3] Any confusion of roles ended abruptly in 1803 when Henry died at the age of only 35. It was thus his brother Edward who, with considerable drive and ability, carried the family and the estate forward into the nineteenth century.

Edward Berkeley Portman I (1771–1823) was a remarkable man, who, after attending St John's College, Cambridge, went on the Grand Tour and in 1798 married Lucy Whitby. Like his father before him he became High Sheriff of Dorset but unlike his father, who never served in Parliament, Edward was elected as member for Boroughbridge in Yorkshire in 1802, and for Dorset in 1806, remaining an active MP for the rest of his life.

## *Family Life*

In February 1791 Anne Mary Portman, one of Edward's sisters, wrote to a Dorset friend, Catherine Bower, providing a vivid glimpse of family life for the Portmans during the London season. 'We went to a large party at Mrs Sturts in St James Square last Tuesday,' she begins. 'A great deal of fine company, the Prince of Wales, Duke of York, & Clarence were there, & Mrs Fitz Herbert who look'd very handsome…' Her letter then continues:

> There was a large Party at the Faro Table; & there is another new Table brought up, called the Rouge & Noir game… I believe we shall go to the Opera next Tuesday, which will be over about eleven o'Clock, & from thence to Mrs Sturts Party. Last Thursday we went to a Play at Covent Garden… The fashions this Year are not much altere'd, as to Caps & Bonnets: the deep veils which some people wear are *frightful*, I have a very moderate one, & find mine *extremely troublesome*. I hope this year will be the last of wearing them… So much for this nonsense – I saw Mrs Baker last week, she was very well, & is at present very busy furnishing her new house in Portman Square. This morning we have about thirty Visits to make, a very unpleasant employment, merely *Form*, & wishing not to find any of the people at home, nothing so troublesome as getting in and out of a Coach every ten minutes… Pray let me hear from you soon.[4]

As the letter suggests, the Portmans had a full social life and lived in considerable style. Anne Mary was writing from what is now 67 Harley Street, the house her father Henry William II had rented as his London home from 1789. Both his sons, Henry and Edward, lived in Portman Square. But when Edward's wife Lucy died in 1812, leaving him with a young family of four sons and three daughters, he decided that he needed a more substantial London base. Bryanston Square was then being planned by James Thompson Parkinson with distinctive columned mansion houses at each corner and also, originally, a larger mansion

Elevation and plans of 38 Bryanston Square by James Thompson Parkinson, 1814. The house was the centrepiece of the square's western side and for many years the London home of the Portman family. It was destroyed by bombing in 1941.
*Image: The Portman Estate*

house forming a centrepiece on either side. Edward took the centre house on the west side, no.38, for which the building agreement, with two fine drawings, has survived.[5] A note of 1815 implies that Parkinson ran into debt and that the house was in fact completed by John White, surveyor of the Portland Estate. At all events the building was finished by 1818 when Edward took up residence there with his second wife, Mary Hulse, whom he had married two years earlier.

## Edward's Death

Edward Berkeley Portman I did not enjoy his new London house for long. He died in Rome of 'inflammation of the lungs' on 19 January 1823 at the early age of 51. His death in a distant land and the subsequent funeral arrangements must have been a considerable ordeal for his family. The Anglican chaplain in Rome recorded that the funeral service was read over Edward's body in Rome before the coffin was shipped home to London. There it went first to Bryanston Square and then, in a three-day procession, to Bryanston where Edward was finally buried on 16 April.

Full details of the duty payable at his death have survived, including inventories of the family's West Country houses at Bryanston, Orchard Portman and Pylle, as well as the new house in Bryanston Square. Perhaps continental travel gave Edward a taste for wine – the cellars at Bryanston Square contained an estimated 120 dozen bottles of wine, while those at Bryanston had no fewer than 652 dozen bottles and a butt of sherry. Edward's estate was valued overall at £45,415, on which duty at 10% was payable.

Receipt for delivery of Edward Berkeley Portman's coffin to the ship taking it home from Italy to London, 1823.
*Image: The Portman Estate*

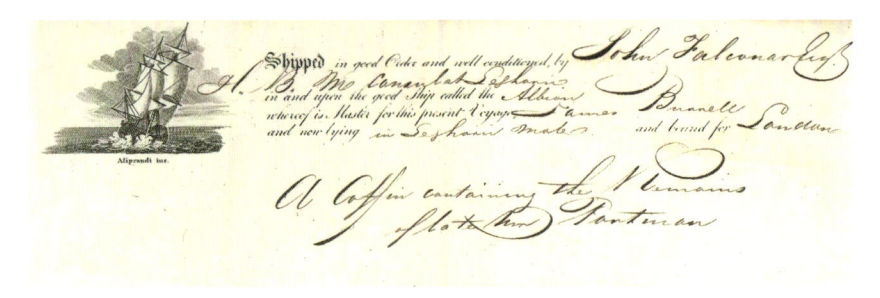

Under his will, Edward set up a trust fund of £70,000 for his children and left the affairs of the estate arranged in a new and businesslike way. No portrait of Edward has been found – which is perhaps an indication of his modesty – but there is no doubt that the estate owed a great deal to his determination and efficiency. His grandfather had set the wheels of the estate's development in motion. His father, though we know little of him as a person, may have had more panache – rebuilding the house at Bryanston as well as creating Portman Square. But it was Edward Berkeley Portman I who set the estate on course for the future.

## The First Lord Portman

When his father died in 1823 Edward Berkeley Portman II (1799–1888) was only 23 years old. He was a notably able and intelligent man who, after attending Eton, graduated in 1821 from Christ Church, Oxford, with first class honours.

Despite his youth, he quickly established himself at the head of the family and also began a long Parliamentary career. At the elections in 1823 he stood as a Whig for his father's old Dorset seat and held it until the Reform Act in 1832. Then, despite the pleas of his constituents to remain a Dorset member, he stood successfully for the new constituency of St Marylebone, resigning in 1833 perhaps because of his numerous family and estate commitments or in expectation of a rumoured peerage.[6]

He had by this time already overseen a number of major developments on the London estate and was well-established as a public figure. Thomas Smith in 1833 chose to dedicate a history of Marylebone to him 'as a humble but hearty tribute to his private worth and public integrity'. He was a man of whom much was expected.

Portrait of Lord Portman by Edward Fancourt, *c.* 1840.
*Image: The Portman Estate*

Portrait of Lady Portman by Edward Fancourt, *c.* 1840.
*Image: The Portman Estate*

In 1827 he married Lady Emma Lascelles, third daughter of the Earl of Harewood, and soon the first of their six children was born. A peerage finally came in 1837 when, on 27 January, he was created 'Baron Portman of Orchard Portman in the County of Somerset'. As if to confirm the family's rising fortunes, Queen Victoria wrote to Lady Portman on 6 July that year inviting her to become a lady of the bedchamber.[7]

Both these appointments may have been influenced by the charismatic figure of Lord Melbourne, the Whig Prime Minister from 1835 to 1841. Lord Portman certainly knew Melbourne and in 1834 had corresponded with him, in his role as Home Secretary, over the demands of the group of Dorset labourers who were soon known as the Tolpuddle Martyrs. Tolpuddle was only 13 miles from Bryanston and Lord Portman was clear that the issues being raised there were 'a mischief and an evil' and that he wanted to 'crush the union'.[8]

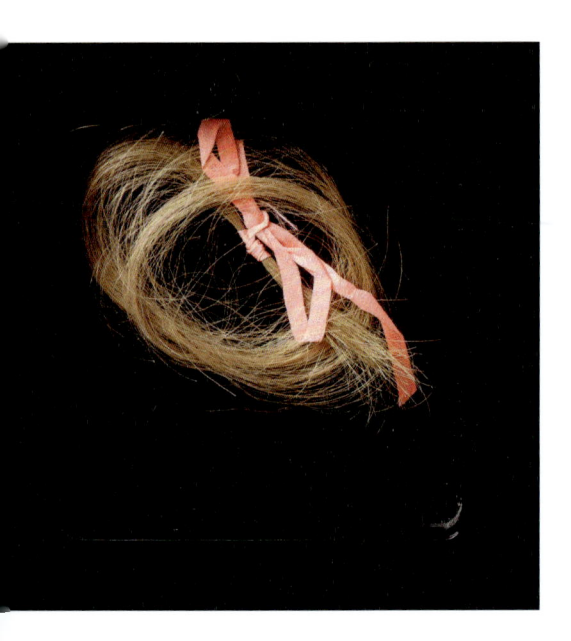

A lock of Queen Victoria's hair given to Lady Portman by the Queen, 6 February 1838.
*Image: The Portman Estate*

## The Flora Hastings Scandal

In 1839 the lives of both Lord and Lady Portman were turned upside down by a scandal concerning Lady Flora Hastings, a lady-in-waiting to the Duchess of Kent, Queen Victoria's mother.

When Lady Flora came back from a visit to Scotland in January 1839 the ladies of the court noticed that she had grown much larger. Tongues wagged, and a few weeks later Queen Victoria herself recorded her suspicion that Lady Flora was 'with child!' In order to be allowed to remain at court Lady Flora had to undergo the indignity of a medical examination, and as one of the Queen's ladies of the bedchamber Lady Portman was closely involved. The medical examination – at which one

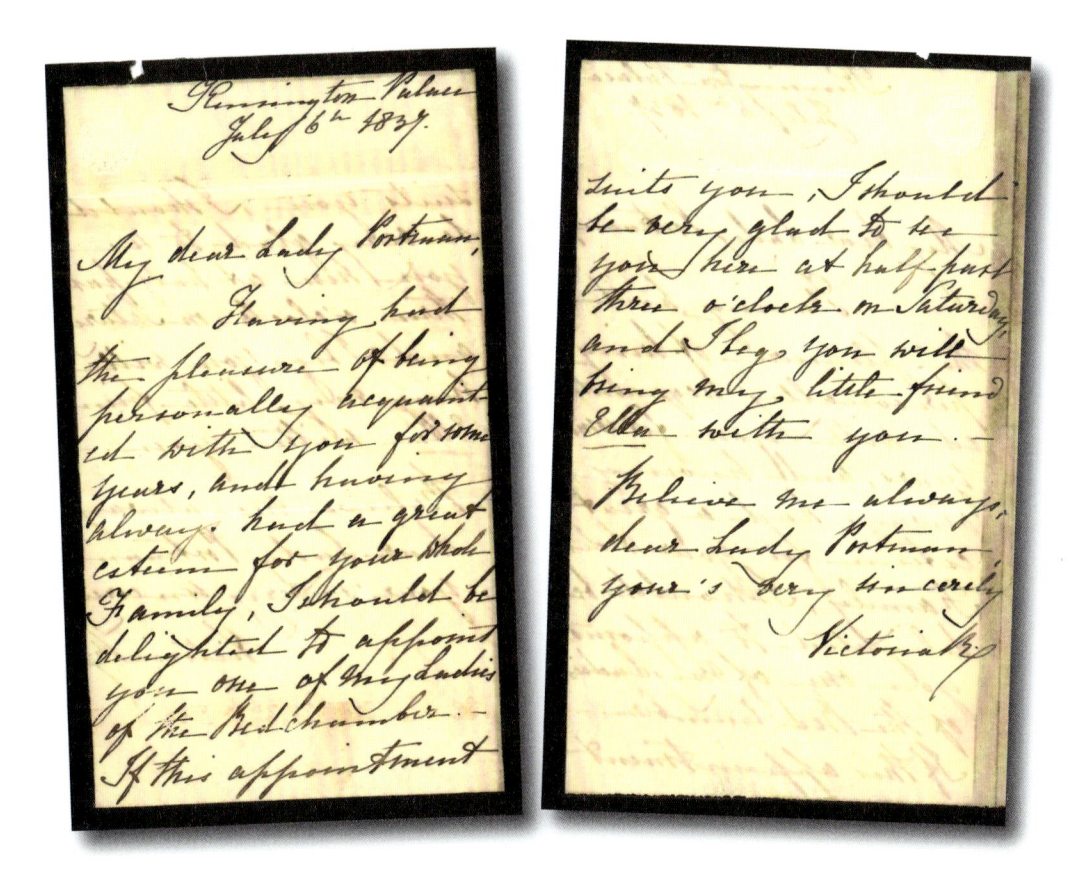

Letter from Queen Victoria to Lady Portman, 6 July 1837, inviting her to become one of her Ladies of the Bedchamber.
*Image: The Portman Estate*

of the doctors was Sir James Clark, who had witnessed the death in Rome of Lord Portman's father – proved conclusively that Lady Flora was not pregnant. But by now her honour was at stake, and she complained bitterly to her brother, the Marquis of Tavistock. He demanded a public apology and came close to challenging Lord Melbourne, the Queen's chief protector, to a duel. When the story reached the newspapers the Queen was hissed in public and arrived at the theatre one evening to be met with the cry 'Dismiss Lady Portman!'

There followed in May the famous Bedchamber Crisis, during which Sir Robert Peel was thwarted in his attempt to form a Tory government by the Queen's refusal to dismiss her Whig ladies of the bedchamber. Melbourne returned as Prime Minister instead. When Lady Flora died of an enlarged liver in July, Melbourne was so nervous of the public reaction that he had the funeral procession leave Buckingham Palace for the journey to Scotland at four in the morning, guarded even at that hour by the police.[9]

The Queen's unpopularity continued for many months, as did press attention. Lord Portman was inevitably drawn into defending his wife and followed the progress of events in newspapers which are still preserved in the estate archives.[10] Queen Victoria's regard for Lady Portman evidently did not diminish. She retained her as a lady of the bedchamber until 1851 and a series of affectionate letters from the Queen has survived in the family papers, together with other pieces of royal memorabilia. Lady Portman died in 1865 at the age of only 55, to be survived for another 23 years by her long-lived husband.

## *Public Service*

Lord Portman's public service was not confined to his membership first of the House of Commons and then of the Lords. For 25 years, from 1839 to 1864, he was Lord Lieutenant of Somerset, and also held other offices reflecting his lifelong interest in agriculture and estate management. He was President of the Royal Agricultural Society in 1846, 1856 and 1862, was appointed a Commissioner and Councillor of the Duchy of Cornwall in 1840 and became a Councillor of the Duchy of Lancaster in 1847. His most significant public appointments came in 1865 when he was made Lord Warden of the Stannaries and High Steward of the Duchy of Cornwall, offices he held for the rest of his life.

A series of letters from Lord Portman to Mr Gladstone, the Prime Minister, confirm his very considerable achievements for the Duchy of

Lancaster and the Duchy of Cornwall. In 1873 his contribution was recognised by the offer of a viscountcy. The offer, Gladstone told him in a letter, was 'in acknowledgement not merely of your high position and long public service, but also and especially of the able and faithful manner in which you have promoted the interests of the Monarchy in connection with the revenues and management of the Duchy of Cornwall.' He added that 'it would have been a real pain to me had I quitted the service of the Queen without tendering to you this slight recognition.'[11]

The next day, writing from Bryanston, Lord Portman replied:

> I feel very deeply the kindness of your letter just received. That you should have thought of me at a time of such deep anxiety is indeed much more than I could have felt I have in any way deserved. I have endeavoured (for 35 years completed) to serve the Queen faithfully in my vocation and have done all that I promised Lord Melbourne I would try to do, in the revival of the Duchy of Cornwall's property, with a success beyond my hopes in 1837. Mainly however I must attribute our success to the steady support given by the Prince Consort to the suggestions I have laid down. I accept the honour which, with the sanction of the Queen, you are so kind as to offer to confer on me... May I hope that you will be so kind as to tender to the Queen my humble duty and my heartfelt thanks...'[12]

Two days later, in a letter written to the MP George Glyn, Lord Portman reflected on whether he should take as his title Viscount Portman of Bryanston in the county of Dorset or of Marylebone in the county of Middlesex. Bryanston won the day, Lord Portman remarking in the letter that 'the former opened my career in Parliament in February 1823... the latter has enabled me to pay off all the debts created by my father and grandfather so that my son will have an estate without a charge.' Those debts arose not least from three mortgages, totalling £45,000, taken out by his father in 1821 to fund a family trust for the benefit of his six younger children. Fifty-two years later the London estate, where a large number of leases were soon to come up for renewal, had more than realised its financial promise.[13]

## A Growing Dynasty

At times during the eighteenth century the continuation of the direct line of the Portman family had depended on the survival of an infant son. During the middle years of the nineteenth century, by contrast, the family grew greatly in size and was soon becoming almost a dynasty, with the first Lord Portman (later 1st Viscount) at its head.

Lord Portman had four sons and two daughters. Neither of his daughters married but two of his sons produced large families. His eldest son, William Henry Berkeley Portman (1829–1919), later the 2nd Viscount, was educated at Eton and at Merton College, Oxford, and was active politically. In 1855 he made an excellent marriage to Mary Selina Charlotte Wentworth Fitzwilliam, heiress of Viscount Milton, with whom he had six sons and four daughters.

The 1st Viscount's second son, Edwin Berkeley Portman (1830–1921), succeeded his brother in 1885 as Liberal MP for North Dorset, holding the seat for seven years. He lived to the age of 91 but had only one

View of Stoke St Mary, *c.* 1910. Stoke St Mary was one of many villages near Taunton where the Portman family continued to be chief landowners until the twentieth century.
*Image: Tom Mayberry*

daughter. Maurice Berkeley Portman (1833–1888), the third son, was an attaché at the British Legation in Mexico from 1853 to 1856 and later moved to Canada where he became a Member of Parliament. He married twice and had a total of six children, the line continuing through Michael Portman, a Lieutenant-Colonel in the 15th/19th Hussars.[14] The 1st Viscount's youngest son, the Revd Walter Berkeley Portman, was rector of Corton Denham in Somerset from 1861 to 1903 and had three sons and a daughter. None of them produced any children but Walter's eldest son, Alan, succeeded him as rector from 1903 to 1925.

The rapid growth of the family depended not just on the children of the first Lord Portman, but on the families of his three brothers and three sisters. Space permits only some of them to be mentioned here though the estate office remains in touch with many descendants.

The brother nearest in age to the 1st Viscount, Henry William Berkeley Portman (1801–1879), became a major in the 7th Hussars and lived in the old Berkeley manor house at Pylle in Somerset. The second of Henry William's three sons, the Revd Henry Fitzhardinge Berkeley Portman, was rector of Pylle from 1866 to 1885 and of Orchard Portman with Thurlbear and Stoke St Mary from 1885 to 1924. The rector's daughter Blanche died in 1962 aged 92, and another daughter, Isobel Grace, died only in 1991 at the great age of 100. She was the last of the family to live at Orchard Portman and is buried there.

Lord Portman's next brother, Wyndham Berkeley Portman (1804–1883), was a captain in the Royal Navy, and his youngest brother, the Revd Fitzhardinge Berkeley Portman (1811–1893), was for 50 years rector of Staple Fitzpaine near Orchard Portman. The right to appoint rectors to parishes owned by the family belonged to Lord Portman as patron. This was part of the accepted way of things in the nineteenth century but was also a great convenience when family members happened to be clergymen in search of livings.

The Revd Fitzhardinge Berkeley Portman (1811–1893). He was rector of Staple Fitzpaine, Somerset, from 1840 to 1893.
*Image: Tom Mayberry*

Several members of the family distinguished themselves in different ways during the late nineteenth and early twentieth centuries. Arthur Portman, a grandson of the 1st Viscount, became editor of *Horse and Hound* in 1890, succeeding his father, Wyndham, who had founded the magazine in 1884. Arthur was said to be the finest shot in the country, and an authority on racing matters as well as a great traveller. He remained editor for 50 years, before being killed, with his wife and six servants, by a bomb which hit 29 Montagu Square in September 1940. His cousin Lionel, one of the three sons of the Revd Walter Berkeley Portman, coxed the Oxford crew to victory in the 50th Boat Race in 1893 and later worked for some years in the East African Colonial Service. He published two books based on his experiences – *Station Studies: the Jottings of an African Official* (1903), and *The Progress of Hugh Rendal: a Public School Story* (1905). These were followed in 1922 by *Three Asses in Bolivia*.

Maurice Vidal Portman (1860–1935), another grandson of the 1st Viscount, had a very unusual career. At the age of only 16 he joined the Indian navy and by 1879 was Officer in Charge of the Andaman Islands. He stayed there for more than 20 years and his obituary in *The Times* called him the 'father' of the Andaman Islanders. Over time he gained their trust, photographing their way of life and writing about them at length. The British Library has almost 500 of his photographs and there are others elsewhere. His obituary also refers to the Secret Service work he undertook during the First World War, but no details are provided or have been discovered since.

One of the most remarkable of the Portmans in this period was the 2nd Viscount's youngest daughter, Mary Isabel Portman (1877–1931). She was a violinist of great ability who was taught by the German virtuoso August Wilhelmj and owned three of the world's most celebrated violins. The first was a Stradivarius of 1722 (her 'thousand guinea violin'), which was probably given to her by her mother. The

Mary Isabel Portman (1877–1931) with her violin, *c.* 1890.
*Image: The Portman Estate*

Schloss Kranzbach in southern Bavaria, commissioned by Mary Portman in 1913.
*Image: © Das Kranzbach Hotel*

others were both made by Guarneri del Gesù, one of them still being known as the 'Mary Portman'. In about 1907 she moved to Berlin and in 1913 commissioned a vast new home, with a concert hall, in the remote countryside of southern Bavaria. The house, designed by the English architect Detmar Blow, was called Schloss Kranzbach and was almost complete when the First World War broke out. But the disruptions of the time meant that Mary was never able to live there.[15]

Mary's introduction to continental Europe was evidently made during two long holidays she and her mother took during the 1890s, the first of them recorded in a long diary illustrated with photographs, watercolours and pressed flowers.[16] Other family members, with a few exceptions, were not notable travellers, though there were some journeys abroad. The 2nd Viscount left diaries of a number of visits that he made to the Continent in his twenties and two of his sons, Edward and Henry, made regular summer fishing trips to Norway. The collection of family papers generously presented to the estate in 2008 by Lady Knutsford includes four albums of photographs of a major trip to the Far East thought to have been made by her grandfather Claud Berkeley Portman, who in 1923 became the 4th Viscount.

## A House in Town

The family's rapid increase in wealth and influence during the nineteenth century led them to seek a series of increasingly grand London homes. In 1818 the 1st Viscount's father, as we have seen, took up residence in a house in the recently-completed Bryanston Square. The 1st Viscount himself lived for some years at 5 Prince's Gate, a mansion on the south

The Reception Room and Drawing Room at Montagu House, Portman Square, photographed by Bedford Lemere, 1894.
*Image: The Portman Estate*

Photograph of one of Lady Portman's garden parties at Montagu House, Portman Square, July 1898. The original caption describes 'a very fashionable crowd, taking tea and discoursing scandal under the trees'.
*Image: © Westminster City Archives*

side of Hyde Park. But when in 1872 the 99-year lease expired on the magnificent Montagu House in Portman Square he was quick to acquire it for his family and to rename it Portman House. After the 1st Viscount's death in 1888 at the age of 89, his son the 2nd Viscount retained the house and in 1894 its sumptuously-furnished rooms were recorded in a wonderful set of photographs by Bedford Lemere.

The house provided an ideal setting for family gatherings such as those that followed the weddings of the 2nd Viscount's daughter Emma Selina (Lena) to the Hon. Ronald Melville in 1885, and that of her younger sister, Susan, to Alan Heber-Percy in 1893. In the 1890s Portman House also hosted a series of garden parties and balls for up to 800 guests at a time.

It was far from London, however, on the ancestral estate at Bryanston in Dorset, that the Portmans created the most prodigious of their family homes.

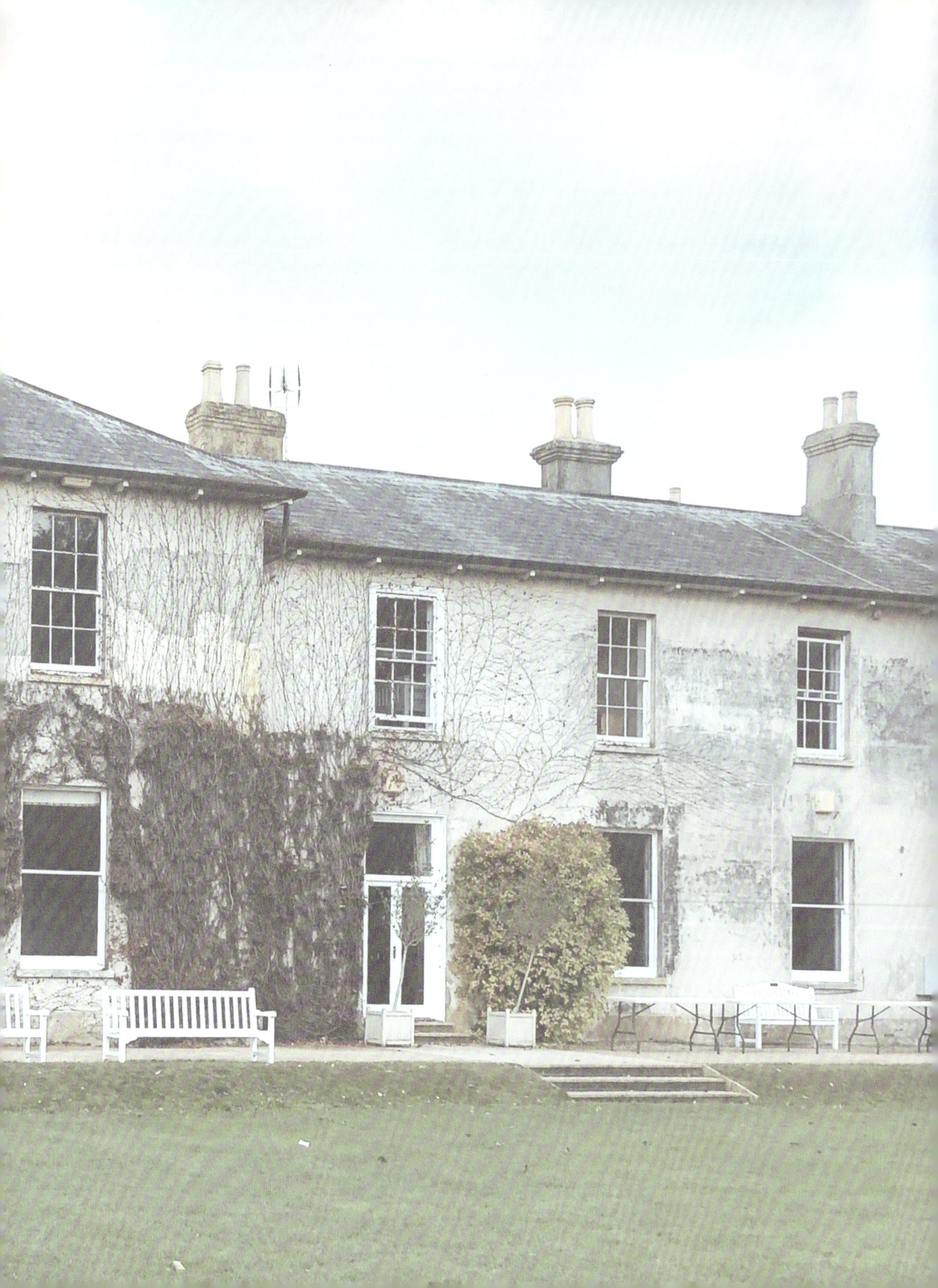

CHAPTER 5

# Dorset Days

*Bryanston in the Time of the First Viscount*

When Edward Berkeley Portman II became head of the family in 1823 the new mansion at Bryanston was already nearly 40 years old. It had by then fully established itself in the affections of the Portmans as the principal setting for their lives outside London and was the place from which they managed their vast farming estates. By 1883 those estates included 24,339 acres in Somerset, 7,798 acres in Dorset and 1,754 acres in Devon.[1]

The 1st Viscount would reflect as an old man on the many challenges that came with his rural inheritance:

> I felt from the first when I saw the mass of dilapidation that was around me that my first duty was to endeavour to revive and restore the estate. I felt that not only was it due to the tenants who occupied farms that buildings should be first thought of and their accommodation sought to be provided, but that those who laboured for them and who earned their bread by the sweat of their brow should have, as soon as possible, better houses to live in… It is perhaps the privilege of an old man sometimes to recall to the thoughts of the younger men

Lord and Lady Portman outside Bryanston House, *c.* 1860. Lord Portman became 1st Viscount Portman in 1874.
*Image: The Portman Estate*

among whom he is spared to live that there were evil days in this country fifty years ago.[2]

Many estate cottages were rebuilt in this period, and the 1st Viscount also undertook a major reorganisation of the farming estate. He amalgamated small farms into larger ones, renewed farmhouses and buildings, and chose tenants who would use the progressive methods of which he was a leading advocate. He created numerous 'model' farms, which employed the latest equipment and techniques, building the most

Knighton House Durweston, Dorset, in 2021.
*Image: Tom Mayberry*

Garden staff at Hestercombe House, Somerset, c. 1910. *Image: The Portman Estate*

ambitious at Bryanston itself as his own home farm.[3] There, in about 1840, a large complex of buildings arose close to the earlier Bryanston Farmhouse. The new buildings were designed to allow intensive feed production for animals on the farm, and included cart sheds, stables, a granary, a mixing house and a steam threshing barn, together with a sawmill, bone mill, malt mill, chaff cutters and corn and cake crushers. At the heart of the farm, in the engine house, was a steam engine – 'the most efficient in the county' – which provided an essential source of power.[4]

In 1880 the home farm at Bryanston was said to be about 1,000 acres in extent, a quarter of it arable, the rest pasture and downland. There were 269 dairy and other cattle (including the high-class pedigree Devons for which Lord Portman was famous), about 1,500 sheep (Southdowns crossed with Hampshires), and a great many 'excellent' pigs. By the end of the century the neglect and dilapidation of earlier times had entirely vanished, even in a period of agricultural depression, and in 1902 Rider Haggard wrote that he had never before seen 'such buildings or cottages' as at Bryanston. 'Everything is managed without thought of cost.'[5]

## Julietta Forrester

Much that is known about life on the Bryanston estate in the second half of the nineteenth century comes from the vivid and voluminous diaries of Julietta Forrester. Her husband James became steward of the estate in 1864 and for the next 43 years was the 'able prime minister in all agricultural matters'[6] to the 1st and 2nd Viscounts.

Julietta's diaries describe the complex, closely-regulated life of the estate, the unpredictability of the largely benevolent Portman family, and her own high-spirited resistance to the limitations placed upon her. Bryanston and the neighbouring Durweston, as Julietta describes them, were the setting for the lives not only of the Portmans themselves but of about 150 estate workers and other staff, including the steward, various foremen, the blacksmith, the huntsman, the head forester, estate labourers, the butler, the housekeeper and the indoor staff.[7] Together they ensured that the work of the home farm was excellently carried out and that the great house was well ordered for the comfort of the extended Portman family and their guests. In addition woodlands were managed, pheasants reared and the horses and hounds kept ready for the hunt.

The routine of the estate year, including weekly attendance at church in Bryanston or Durweston, was punctuated by more vivid events. They included the annual rook shoot, audit dinners in Blandford or elsewhere and, especially, the festivities at Christmas. Often the River Stour froze over at just the right moment and people of all kinds, with Lord Portman's consent, went skating on sometimes dangerously thin ice.[8] On Christmas Eve carol singers did their rounds from door to door. And in the days after Christmas, tenants and workers were invited to the mansion to see the Christmas tree lit with candles. In 1876 it stood 17 feet high and was placed where it would be reflected in two large mirrors. 'The effect was charming,' Julietta wrote. Christmas was anticipated for other reasons as well. It was at this time of year that the Portmans distributed food and clothing to their tenants, including in 1872 'jackets… to the poor women'.[9]

The steady procession of visitors and house guests received by Lord Portman included some

Photograph of Julietta Forrester (1856–1917), *c.* 1885.
*Image: The Portman Estate*

Photograph of James Forrester, Julietta's husband and steward of the estate from 1864 to 1907.
*Image: The Portman Estate*

who were never forgotten. On 23 August 1882, while a cricket match was in progress on the ground at Bryanston, the Prime Minister Mr Gladstone called to visit. Julietta positioned herself on the carriage drive for his departure and saw 'a thin, pale old man sitting low, looking very serious under a big old-fashioned hat.'[10] The visit on 24 January 1884 of the Prince and Princess of Wales left an even greater impression. The church bells rang, and the Royal party, consisting of 11 or 12 on horseback followed by two open carriages, made its way down the long approach to the mansion. The Prince and Princess inspected Lord Portman's hounds approvingly and the Prince exclaimed 'What a pretty place this is'.[11] It would be almost twenty-six years before he paid a return visit, by that time as King Edward VII.

But the occasion which surpassed all others in local memory was the family celebration in 1877 to mark the coming of age of Edward (Teddy) Portman, Lord Portman's eldest grandson. After a loyal address was read to 'Mr Edward' on the grand staircase in the mansion, a thousand guests gathered in a marquee erected in a neighbouring meadow. There, a London caterer with 150 assistants had set out a 'princely feast' on tables decorated with gilt vases and figures bearing fruit and flowers. In two other tents 1,200 children were entertained to tea, after which they marched in procession past the mansion and were each presented with a book. By evening the torrential rain which had marred the day was over and the crowds

'The three generations', 1877, showing, from left to right, Edward Berkeley Portman, 1st Viscount, Edward William Berkeley Portman (Teddy), the 2nd Viscount's eldest son, and William Henry Berkeley Portman, 2nd Viscount.
*Image: The Portman Estate*

Hestercombe House during the coming of age celebrations of Edward William Berkely Portman in 1877.
*Images: South West Heritage Trust*

gathered for a grand firework display. It ended with a set piece which spelt out in the darkness the words 'Long Live E. W. B. Portman'.

A week later, in the presence of thousands more, the whole extraordinary event was repeated at Hestercombe, the Somerset mansion just west of Taunton which the Portmans had acquired in 1872. It was

The Portman family at Bryanston on the coming of age of Edward William Berkeley Portman, July 1877.
*Image: South West Heritage Trust*

there that Teddy Portman would make his home, ensuring its fame by commissioning Sir Edwin Lutyens and Gertrude Jekyll to create its celebrated formal gardens. But the hopes so extravagantly expressed for him at his coming of age were destined to remain unfulfilled. He died at Hestercombe in 1910, aged 56, and never succeeded to the title.[12]

The 1st Viscount, in his old age, retained a lively interest in the work and welfare of his estates. In April 1883, after a long illness, he rode out in his donkey chair to see the new bull James Forrester had bought, and in June lived up to his reputation as an improving landowner by commissioning the installation of a turbine wheel for Bryanston. When Joseph Arch, the leader of the National Agricultural Labourers Union, addressed a meeting in Blandford the following year, Julietta thought that 'a Revolution cannot be far off.'[13] But even in the midst of general agricultural depression, the Portman estates seemed more than usually immune from wider economic and social pressures.

Edward William Berkeley Portman (1856–1911), (Teddy), the eldest son of the 2nd Viscount. He lived at Hestercombe House, near Taunton.
*Image: Tom Mayberry*

It was on the afternoon of 19 November 1888, while Julietta Forrester was making nightshirts at home, that news reached her from the estate yard that old Lord Portman had died that afternoon. Only the butler and the housekeeper were with him at the end to hear his last words as he fainted away: 'I cannot see – I am dying.' This intelligent, able and broadly benevolent man had been perhaps the most remarkable of the Portmans since the seventeenth century, and his death at a great age made a deep impression. George Guy tolled the passing bell, and on 21 November villagers processed through the mansion to pay their last respects to Lord Portman as he lay in his cedar inner coffin.[14]

Three days later tenants from Dorset and Somerset gathered at the mansion for a luncheon which included 'soup, meat, game, pastry, sweets and fruit'. At one o'clock the bells at Bryanston, Blandford, Durweston and Pimperne began to toll, and in the Portman chapel, which was draped in black, the vault had been opened for a final time to receive a head of the family. The largest wreath, of chrysanthemums and violets, was from the Prince of Wales, and included a message in his own hand that read 'A token of sincere respect and regard from Albert Edward'.[15]

The passing of the old order at Bryanston was destined to be marked more emphatically than anyone could have guessed. On 6 June 1889, less than seven months after the death of the 1st Viscount, surveyors arrived from London to mark out the site of a new Bryanston on high ground north-west of the Wyatt mansion. Julietta Forrester, visiting the site in July, recorded her opinion succinctly in her diary: 'a big Folly!'[16]

## The New Bryanston

William Henry Berkeley Portman, 2nd Viscount Portman, was 59 years old when he inherited. He shared his father's wide-ranging agricultural interests and was legendary in the hunting field: for 61 years, from 1858, he was Master of the Portman Hunt, whose country covered a large part of east Dorset. Like his father he was an active politician. He was Member of Parliament for Shaftesbury from 1852 to 1857, and for Dorset from 1857 to 1885, shocking the political world in 1890 when, as a Member of the House of Lords, he abandoned the Liberals for the Conservatives over the question of Irish Home Rule.[17] In the year he succeeded he also became the first chairman of Dorset County Council, only giving up the post in 1917, aged 88, when deafness meant he could no longer hear what was being said.[18]

For many years before his father's death William and his wife Mary

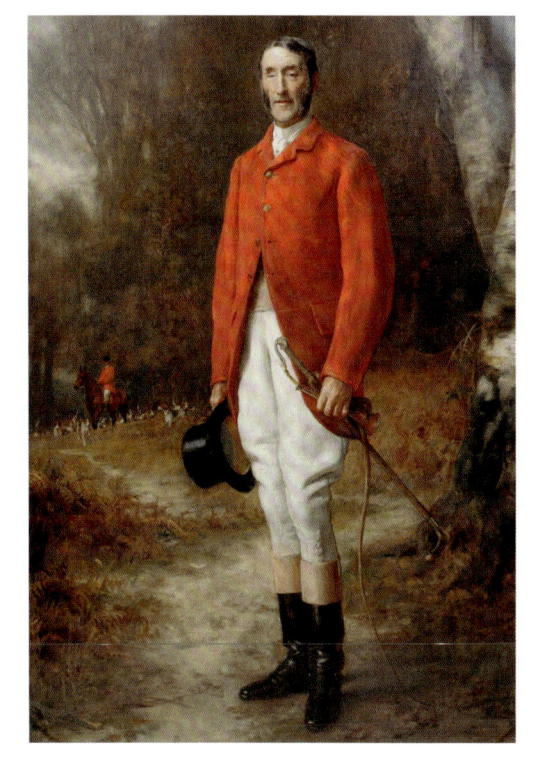

Left: Portrait of Mary Selina Charlotte Wentworth Fitzwilliam (1836–1899), 2nd Viscountess Portman, by Charles West Cope, 1897.
Right: William Henry Berkeley Portman, 2nd Viscount Portman, as Master of the Portman Hunt.
*Images: The Portman Estate*

Fitzwilliam lived in relative modesty at Knighton House, Durweston, a short distance from Bryanston. The large family they raised there included four sons who would eventually succeed to the title, and it must have seemed that for the first time in several generations the continuance of the Portman line and name was beyond any doubt. The family was also far wealthier now than it had ever been, especially when the renewal of long leases on the London estate brought an enormous windfall income in 1888.[19]

The creation of the new Bryanston thus emerged from the opportunity provided by great wealth, but must also have expressed the family's high and growing sense of its late Victorian status. To Nikolaus Pevsner the new Bryanston proclaimed 'the pride of the well-born and super-wealthy'. To Andrew Saint the Portmans, by building their prodigy

The entrance front and garden front of the new Bryanston, from *The Builder*, 5 August 1899. *Images: Tom Mayberry*

house, 'joined the great club of European aristocracy, not knowing that its days were numbered'. Saint also suggests that Bryanston expressed Lord Portman's hopes of a ministerial appointment. In reality, his motives cannot be known for certain, though his wife reputedly had a crucial part in the decision to rebuild. Memories of the Fitzwilliam family home in Yorkshire, the palatial Wentworth Woodhouse, must have made the Wyatt mansion seem a modest building by comparison. Worse still, the old house was said to be damp because of its low-lying site near the river.[20]

As architect for the new mansion Lord Portman chose Richard Norman Shaw (1831–1912), a man possessing one of the most inventive architectural minds of his generation. Shaw made his name from the 1870s onwards as the creator of houses, both in town and country, which were often in the Queen Anne style. His work was characterised by ingenious planning, excellent craftsmanship and a readiness, as at Bryanston, to use modern materials, such as iron and steel girders. Shaw visited Lord Portman at Bryanston in the spring of 1889 and saw the intended site for the new house. In initial conversations Shaw talked of 'mullioned windows', and was evidently suggesting a building in his 'Old English' manner. But by the time he wrote to Lord Portman on 28 March, he was proposing instead a building which used the classical language of the Wyatt mansion. Apart from any other considerations, that would make it possible to re-use elements of the old house 'such as *all* doors, chimney pieces &c.'

The plans as soon agreed were for a vast brick-built symmetrical house in a classical Wren-derived style. Inspiration from the Loire chateau of Menars has also been suggested. Shaw wanted the mansion to be 'simple & dignified', and as far as possible he also sought compactness. But the scale remained overwhelming, and presumably reflected his client's view that this was a house intended not for domesticity but as a grand public stage. In the ten years after the house was completed, however, there were evidently only a handful of occasions when it fulfilled such a role, and at the housewarming in 1895 those who attended were the same minor gentry and local clergy who had happily crowded into the old mansion by the river. Rural Dorset could never be London, and this was one of the conundrums at the heart of the new Bryanston. But while the money lasted it hardly mattered.[21]

Bryanston remains today an unforgettable architectural statement. The immediate impression made by the house is of immense scale and of a vivid, restless contrast between the red brick of the walls and the white Portland-stone dressings. The entrance front is dominated by a high central block with a hipped roof, towering chimneys and a vast front door. Flanking the central block are lower projecting wings which complete three sides of a courtyard. On the garden front, where the land falls away, the mansion reaches its full width of 305 feet, the central block projecting forward to look out over the valley of the River Stour.

The architectural drama continues inside. A grand entrance hall leads to a central top-lit saloon which in turn stands at the mid-point of a corridor, 100 yards long, running the entire width of the house. Bryanston's three enormous reception rooms look out on the garden and contain plasterwork in an eighteenth-century style, as well as the neo-classical chimney pieces saved from the Wyatt mansion. Though the

The central corridor in the new Bryanston House, completed by the architect Richard Norman Shaw in 1894.
*Image: The Portman Estate*

rooms are grandly impressive, it is difficult to imagine them as places for living, and only in some of the less public spaces, such as Lord Portman's study, is the overbearing scale reduced to more manageable proportions.

The great task of building the mansion, which lasted more than five years and cost an estimated £250,000, was given to the London firm of Holland, Hannen and Cubitts. After the site was marked out in June 1889, initial progress was interrupted in November when the workers demanded a penny increase on their hourly pay of 3½*d*. Thereafter the massive project was taken steadily forward by a workforce which ranged in size from 200 to 300 men, and which in its final stages included a 'small army of Italian decorators'. At Christmas 1892 Lord Portman allowed beef to be given to the workforce, Julietta Forrester remarking that they 'seemed eager as wild beasts at feeding time at the Zoo', though they remained 'good tempered and well behaved'.[22]

The main reception room at Bryanston House, Dorset, looking towards the fireplace, 1899.
*Image: Historic England*

Julietta took a keen interest in the progress of the works, especially when Romano-British finds, including human burials, were revealed in the process. In May 1893 she recorded the arrival of two great boilers for the mansion's electric plant, one of them weighing 19 tons, and in November noted that the dynamo had been tested for the first time. She visited the mansion that month and found the works being 'pushed at a great rate'. By now it was possible to reach the top of the building where Julietta was 'much pleased with the rooms'.[23]

Lord Portman slept in his unfinished mansion for the first time on 16 June 1894, and by late October the remaining workforce was at last departing. Norman Shaw's commission was effectively complete and had required over 6 million bricks, 58,000 cubic feet of stone and 6,480 cwt of girders.[24] He was never permitted to carry out his intended scheme for the gardens and grounds. Instead the Portmans took control, one often-told story describing how Lady Portman directed part of the landscaping from an upper window of the mansion. She would signal by dropping her handkerchief when the gardener reached the place where the next tree should be planted. While Bryanston and its setting were being brought to completion, the old mansion by the river was languishing. Finally, late in February 1896, demolition began, the stone being used to create Bryanston's ambitious new church of St Martin.[25]

The public inauguration of the house began on 5 November 1894 when the opening meet of the Portman Hunt gathered in the courtyard. On 18 April 1895 a servants' ball took place, and five days later was the housewarming ball itself. Julietta Forrester was perplexed and angry that she and her husband were not invited to join the 300 guests. Instead she walked out in the darkness to see the great house lit by electricity and the steady procession of carriages arriving at the door. Some of them were, she said, 'very mean looking turn-outs – clergymen's shabby covered vehicles and big broken-winded horses.' Inside the mansion the head gardener, Mr Allsop, had provided floral decorations of 'surpassing beauty'. Palms, lilies, ferns and azaleas filled the rooms, together with baskets of scarlet geraniums. Dancing began at 10 o'clock to the music of a London band and continued till three in the morning. In February the following year a second ball took place, but the guest list, with a few exceptions, remained provincial, and could not compare with Lady Portman's London ball held in June. On that occasion, at Portman Square, Lady Hertford attended in 'a quantity of diamonds' and Lady Ilchester wore emeralds of 'immense size'.[26]

The Portman Hunt gathered in the courtyard at Bryanston.
*Image: The Portman Estate*

## *The End of an Era*

On 4 January 1899, just as Julietta Forrester and her husband were finishing their breakfast, news was brought from the mansion that Lady Portman had died in her sleep, a few days short of her 63rd birthday. Julietta hurried to the post office to get someone to toll the bell, and three days later at Durweston the Portman family gathered for the funeral. Though Lord Portman would marry again in 1908, aged almost 79, the loss of his formidable first wife was a severe blow both to him and to the life of Bryanston. As he entered his long old age he may at last have recognised that the ambitions embodied by Bryanston were never likely to be fulfilled.

    The house and estate continued to be managed lavishly in the early twentieth century. At the mansion Mrs Turnbull, the housekeeper, Mr Sewell, the head butler, and twelve housemaids ensured that the household ran efficiently. On the estate it was said that the senior staff 'all had excellent jobs always dressed in their best suits with no one to bother them, so long as the wheels kept moving'. The tenants, though their wages were low, regarded Lord Portman as a good landlord, and the new Lady Portman as a 'good Christian lady' who did much amongst the poor. Deer roamed free in Bryanston park and peacocks in the gardens and grounds.[27] It was to this tranquil aristocratic kingdom that in December 1909 Edward VII, accompanied by his mistress Alice Keppel, paid a short visit while staying nearby. It was perhaps the only moment in the history of the new mansion when the idea of Bryanston and the reality briefly coincided.[28]

On his 89th birthday in July 1918 Lord Portman received a warmly personal letter from George V offering him the king's personal order, the GCVO. It was, the king said:

> … a mark of my high appreciation of one who having lived in five successive Reigns has rendered valuable service to his Country, and as a great landowner both in London and in the West of England, has given an example of high minded, disinterested devotion to duty.[29]

The GCVO awarded by King George V to the 2nd Viscount Portman on his 89th birthday, July 1918.
*Image: The Portman Estate*

Sir Leslie Ward's 'Spy' cartoon showing the 2nd Viscount Portman as 'The Old Master', 1898.
*Image: Tom Mayberry*

On 16 October 1919 Lord Portman, aged 90, died suddenly at his town house in Portman Square, having recently returned from shooting in Scotland. They brought him home to Bryanston one last time and for three days his coffin rested in the extraordinary house described in an obituary as his 'great Dorsetshire palace'. Then, surrounded by family, friends, staff and tenants, he was buried next to his first wife in the churchyard at Durweston. No one may have realised it then, but Bryanston's great days were now drawing swiftly to a close.[30]

BLANDFORD SQUARE
Portman Nursery
DORSET SQUARE
BRYANSTONE SQUARE
MONTAGUE SQUARE
PORTMAN SQUARE
STANHOPE SQUARE
CONNAUGHT SQUARE
St. George's Burial Ground
St. John's Church
Bentinck Chapel
Cow Yard
Workhouse
St. Mary le Bone
Paddington and St. George's Burying Ground
The Holme
South Villa
Cornwall Terrace
Clarence Terrace
Park Terrace
Alpha Road
Alpha Place
Alpha Cottages
Lisson Grove
Church Street
Salisbury Street
Devonshire St.
Stephens St.
Great James Street
Bell Street
Chapel Street
Upper York Street
York Street
Crawford Street
Dorset Street
Paddington Street
Blandford St.
King Street
George Street
Upper George Str.
Upper Berkeley Str.
Berkeley Street
Upper Seymour Street
Seymour Place
Bryanstone Street
Portman Street
Orchard St.
Baker Street
York Place
Gloucester Place
Montague Place
Dorset Place
Upper Baker Street
New Road
Manchester Street
Edgware Road
Oxford Road
Queen Street
Nutford Place
Cambridge Terrace
Connaught Place
Hyde Park Terrace
Hyde Park St.
Albion Street
Upper Berkeley Street
Oxford

CHAPTER 6
# The Growth of the London Estate, 1824–1919

## An Expanding City

The stability which the Portman Family achieved during the lives of the 1st and 2nd Viscounts was in contrast to the enormous changes taking place on the London estate. A major reason for those changes was the increase in London's population during the nineteenth and early twentieth centuries. In 1801, when the first census was compiled, there were nearly one million people living in the capital. By 1921 the total was approaching eight million. The increase in Marylebone itself was almost as striking and a population of 64,000 in 1801 rose to 162,000 in 1861, remaining at over 130,000 for the next 40 years. Such growth was far greater than has been experienced more recently.

By the 1820s, as has already been seen, the Portman estate was largely complete south of the New Road (called Marylebone Road from 1857), and included Portman, Manchester, Montagu and Bryanston squares. As late as 1800, however, the area to the north was still a place where Londoners could escape from the bustle of the streets to rural walks and scattered taverns. There were also some fine villas, with gardens and lawns, to complete a picture in which 'all the elegances of the town and all the beauties of the country' were combined.[1]

The pressure for change could not be avoided for long. Immediately north of the New Road Dorset Square was built in 1812–26, and was

Above and facing: two watercolours by T. Paul Fisher showing the junction of Lisson Grove and the New Road (Marylebone Road), 1849, in summer and winter. The entrance to the Grammar School was through the stone gateway on the right.
*Images: Courtesy of Sotheby's Picture Library*

soon joined by Blandford and Harewood squares. The fashionable credentials of this part of the estate were never secure and suffered greatly when in 1899 Marylebone Station was opened. There was even less pretence of fashionable living in the north-western corner of the estate, south of the Regent's Canal and east of the Edgware Road. This was part of the area called Lisson Grove (named after the manor of Lilestone) where the effects of a rising population and of often terrible poverty became inescapably clear during the nineteenth century.

## Lisson Grove

The earliest development at Lisson Grove was south of today's Ashmill Street. A small number of streets had been leased there to the Baker family and following completion of the Regent's Canal in 1820 houses and courts for the very poor were built. They had rateable values as low as £3 a year and quickly became overpopulated as well as a major health problem. The main area of development on the Lisson Grove section of the estate was further north. Led by the architect James Thompson Parkinson, building gathered pace during the 1820s and in a period of little more than a decade, as a map of 1834 demonstrates, almost the entire area was built up. Part of the development consisted of modest middle class terraces, but in streets closer to the Edgware Road

Detail from a map of Marylebone by B. R. Davies, F. A. Bartlett and John Britton, 1834. The red line marks the boundary of the estate.
*Image: © Westminster City Archives*

the housing was again of a very different kind. In 1833 Thomas Smith described it as follows:

> The mass of buildings and streets from the Edgware Road to Lisson Grove eastwards…are occupied by the working classes: houses of cheap rent appear to have been the object of the builders; and the principle of speculation has been to take large tracts of ground by the acre, and to crowd as many streets and alleys into them as possible, in order to create so many feet lineal to underlet for building; and the fruit of the speculation is the sale of the increased ground rents.[2]

When in 1874 the medical officer of the Board of Health reported on tenements in Marylebone parish, conditions were desperate. One tenement containing 19 rooms was occupied by 47 people:

> Every part of this miserable abode is in a ruinous and dilapidated condition: the flooring of the rooms and staircases is worn into holes, and broken away; the plaster is crumbling from the walls; the roofs let in the wind and rain; the drains are very defective; and the general aspect of the place is one of extreme wretchedness.[3]

Towards the end of the century Frederick Hunt, agent of the estate, gave evidence to the Royal Commission on the Housing of the Working Classes, 1884–5, and to the Select Committee on Town Holdings, 1887. After decades of government inaction, searching questions were now being asked about London's slums, including those in Lisson Grove. Hunt, in his evidence, explained the operation of the leasehold system, itself one of the reasons for slum housing. The major estates, it was clear, were unable to control subletting or to enforce repairs and, apart from a few attempts at legislation, philanthropic organisations such as the Improved Industrial Dwellings Company and the Peabody Trust were taking the lead in improving living conditions.

Particular concern for the plight of women and children was reflected in the many voluntary organisations established on the estate during the nineteenth century. Only some of them can be mentioned here. In 1847 the Samaritan Hospital for Women and Children opened in Lower Seymour Street (now Wigmore Street), and in 1875 it was joined there by a night home for girls and unmarried women 'of good character'. The New Hospital for Women, which opened in Seymour Street in 1866, moved to new premises in Marylebone Road nine years later, and in 1885 the Marylebone Home for Girls, which opened at 14 Old Quebec Street in 1883, also moved to Marylebone Road. It provided for poor and orphaned girls from the workhouse.[4] But charitable effort could do little to protect the most vulnerable, and in 1885 Lisson Grove made national headlines. W. T. Stead, the crusading editor of the *Pall Mall Gazette*, 'paid' £5 for the 13-year-old Eliza Armstrong in Charles Street, just outside the Portman estate, in order to highlight the scandal of child prostitution. As a result the age of consent was raised from 13 to 16 and Charles Street was demolished, to be rebuilt as Ranston Street by the social reformer Octavia Hill. Stead himself was sent to prison for three months, while Eliza Armstrong's story became the inspiration for George Bernard Shaw's Eliza Doolittle in his play *Pygmalion*.

Extract from Charles Booth's 'Poverty Map 7', 1889. Most of wealthy Marylebone is coloured yellow and red, but much of the Lisson Grove area is blue, dark blue or even black, indicating poverty and crime.
*Image:* © *London School of Economics and Political Science*

Probably influenced partly by Octavia Hill, the Portman estate increasingly took a direct role in improving living conditions. In the 1880s Frederick Hunt negotiated the sale to the Artizans', Labourers' and General Dwellings Company (ALGDC) of a large piece of land at Lisson Grove. It was to be the site of the biggest block of artisans' dwellings so far built in London and in June 1888 was opened as Portman Buildings by Lord Rosebery, Gladstone having declined the invitation. The ALGDC was founded in 1867 and had already built three artisans' estates in different parts of London. But this was their first venture into 'block' building as it was called. In the course of the next two years Hunt negotiated two further agreements with the ALGDC, on generous terms, to build Seymour Buildings in Seymour Place and Wendover Buildings in Chiltern Street.

By 1898–9, when Charles Booth, himself a tenant of the estate, was researching his monumental survey *Life and Labour of the People in London*, the evidence of poverty in Lisson Grove was still plentiful. He gave graphic descriptions of drunkenness, street fighting and prostitution, and summed up his impressions in these words:

> In street after street evil specimens of womankind shuffle along with head wrapped in a shawl, or lean out of windows, or stand gossiping at the open doors. Evil-looking, idle, hulking lads are not an uncommon sight; children who ought to be at school are playing about in the streets; and the houses look filthy without and within.[5]

Those interviewed by Booth and his assistants were nevertheless of the view that conditions were much better than they had been 20 years earlier. That was largely due to the on-going demolition of the worst of the tenements and their replacement by blocks, a process widely approved as one of the Portman estate's enlightened policies. Even so, the very poorest members of society, who were unable to afford the modest rents charged in these blocks, were forced to live wherever they could, often moving from the centre of London and thus reducing the immediate pressure on accommodation. For all of London's private estates the blocks policy thus combined philanthropy with self-interest because it tended to displace the most disadvantaged.

Living conditions in Lisson Grove were to remain a serious concern well into the twentieth century, but the 2nd Viscount faced the problem imaginatively, working with London County Council and St Marylebone Borough Council to achieve pioneering results. Almost none of the buildings which were once the slums of Marylebone have survived until today, and most that were built on Portman land were eventually replaced by council housing.

## From Waxworks to Schools

On both sides of the New Road, developments during the nineteenth century related to much more than housing. At Church Street in Lisson Grove, for example, the Portman Market became a major addition to the street scene in 1832, and fulfilled an ambition which had gone unrealised 50 years earlier near Manchester Square. The market required two Acts of Parliament and although it was located close to centres of high population it was never an unqualified success. In 1900 it was completely rebuilt and given a magnificent central dome, but this new market failed after only six years and the building was later used as a garage. The market did, however, give the area a special character which lives on in Church Street with its mass of colourful stalls.

Perhaps unexpectedly, the Lisson Grove area was also the home of several small theatres. Many were short-lived but one of them lasted for over a century until it was severely damaged by bombing in 1941. This was the Theatre Royal, Church Street, which had a number of different names during its life. For two years, from 1836 to 1837, it was actually called the Portman Theatre, but ended its days as the Royal West London. It was there in 1904 that Charlie Chaplin, aged 15, appeared in his earliest stage role as Billy in William Gillette's *Sherlock Holmes*.

Spectacle of a different kind was available in a vast building on the west side of Baker Street. This was the Baker Street Bazaar (until 1833 the stables of the Life Guards Regiment) where on the first floor Madame Tussaud installed her famous waxworks in 1835. Having

Watercolour by Robert Schnebbelie of the Portman Market, 1834. The market is on the left. St Matthew's Church, Penfold Street, originally planned as a theatre, is on the right.
*Image: © Westminster City Archives*

*View from the stage of the Theatre Royal, Church Street, 1845. Image: © Westminster City Archives*

arrived in England in 1802 she spent more than 30 years touring the country until she found a long-term home for the exhibition. By the 1870s the 'gorgeous apartment' at Baker Street contained more than 300 waxworks, including William the Conqueror, Lord Nelson and Queen Victoria. The 'Chamber of Horrors', viewable for an extra charge, was also an essential part of the displays and included 'some of the greatest criminals of the age'. When the exhibition moved to Marylebone Road in 1884 the former premises were renamed the Portman Rooms and were used for a variety of public events. From 1839 to 1861 the ground floor spaces were the setting for the annual shows of the Royal Smithfield Club, and it was there that the 1st Viscount won many medals for his prize cattle from Bryanston.[6]

As the estate expanded during the nineteenth century additional churches were provided. Just beyond the estate's eastern boundary the new St Marylebone parish church was built in 1817 to the classical designs of Thomas Hardwick. St Mary's, Bryanston Square, the setting for many Portman baptisms, marriages and funerals, was built by the architect Robert Smirke in 1823, and gave a striking focal point to the long view from Great Cumberland Place. Like Christ Church, Cosway

The Baker Street Bazaar, 1839.
*Image: © Westminster City Archives*

Street, designed by Thomas Hardwick and completed in 1824 by his son Philip, St Mary's was a so-called Waterloo or Commissioners' church, paid for mainly with money voted by Parliament. The Aenon Baptist Chapel was built in Church Street in 1830 and lasted until the 1950s. Several other churches were built nearby to meet the demands of the Church Street community and St Edward's Roman Catholic Convent in Harewood Place dates from as long ago as 1850. A large Presbyterian church was founded in George Street in 1843, and in 1870 the first synagogue on the estate, the West London Reform Synagogue, opened in Upper Berkeley Street. That marked the beginning of a local connection with the Jewish community which remains strong.

Many churches did not survive the Second World War but two that have remained deserve special notice. St Cyprian's, Clarence Gate, was completed in 1903 to the designs of Sir Ninian Comper. It is tucked away behind Park Road and is a wonderfully light-filled building in a late gothic style. The Church of the Annunciation, Bryanston Street, is

Drawing by William Prinsep of St Mary's Church, Bryanston Square, seen from Great Cumberland Place, 1834. (From The Diary of William Tayler, Footman, 1837, ed. Dorothy Wise, 1998.)
Image: © Westminster City Archives

quite different in mood. Designed by Sir Walter Tapper in Edwardian gothic, it was completed in 1914 on the site of the eighteenth-century Quebec Chapel. Both St Cyprian's and the Church of the Annunciation were created for High Church Anglican congregations. As a conservative churchman the 1st Viscount had opposed the building of St Cyprian's, but the more liberal 2nd Viscount agreed to them both.

New elementary schools also met the needs of a growing population. The estate and the Portman family had always been closely associated with the Western National School which was built in 1824 at the same time as St Mary's Church, Bryanston Square. In 1861 the rector of St Mary's, the Revd John Hampden Gurney, opened another school in what is now Hampden Gurney Street, and in Nutford Place a school was founded at the same time as the new church of St Luke. The church was built in thanksgiving that the district had escaped the effects of cholera in 1849.[7]

St Marylebone Grammar School, founded in 1792 near Fitzroy Square as the Philological School, moved first to Nutford Place and in 1827 to a site at the junction of Lisson Road and Marylebone Road. Its library, added thirty years later, looks like a Victorian gothic church and is still a prominent feature of the area. After a long fight the Grammar School itself was forced to close in 1981, its former pupils having by then included Len Deighton, Professor Eric Hobsbawm, Jerome K. Jerome, Bertram Mills and the first Viscount Rothermere – a splendidly contrasting group.[8]

## A Transport Revolution

Marylebone led the way in improving the capital's transport links when in 1829 London's first bus service, operating along the New Road between Paddington and the Bank, was opened by George Shillibeer. His horses were stabled behind the Yorkshire Stingo pub, just outside the estate at the top of Seymour Place. In 1863 the same route was followed by the world's first underground railway, the Metropolitan, and in 1893, in spite of considerable opposition, Parliament agreed to the construction of Marylebone Station, which opened six years later. To accommodate the station 14 acres, comprising Blandford Square and Harewood Square, were compulsorily purchased from the estate for £260,000. The new station became the London terminus of the Great Central Railway (until 1897 called the Manchester, Sheffield and Lincolnshire Railway, also widely known as the 'Money Sunk and Lost').

In 1899 and again in 1910 Baker Street Station was enlarged to accommodate the Bakerloo Railway, and in 1900 the Central London Railway, now the Central Line, opened its station at Marble Arch. The three associated land sales realised a further £80,000 and though it was always rare for the estate to part with freehold land these were occasions when there was no choice.

## Managing the Estate

Among those who served as agents for the London estate during the lives of the 1st and 2nd Viscounts two names stand out. In 1834 Philip Hardwick, member of a distinguished architectural dynasty, succeeded Thomas Wilson in the post. Hardwick, like his father Thomas and son Philip Charles, was a prolific architect of buildings in London

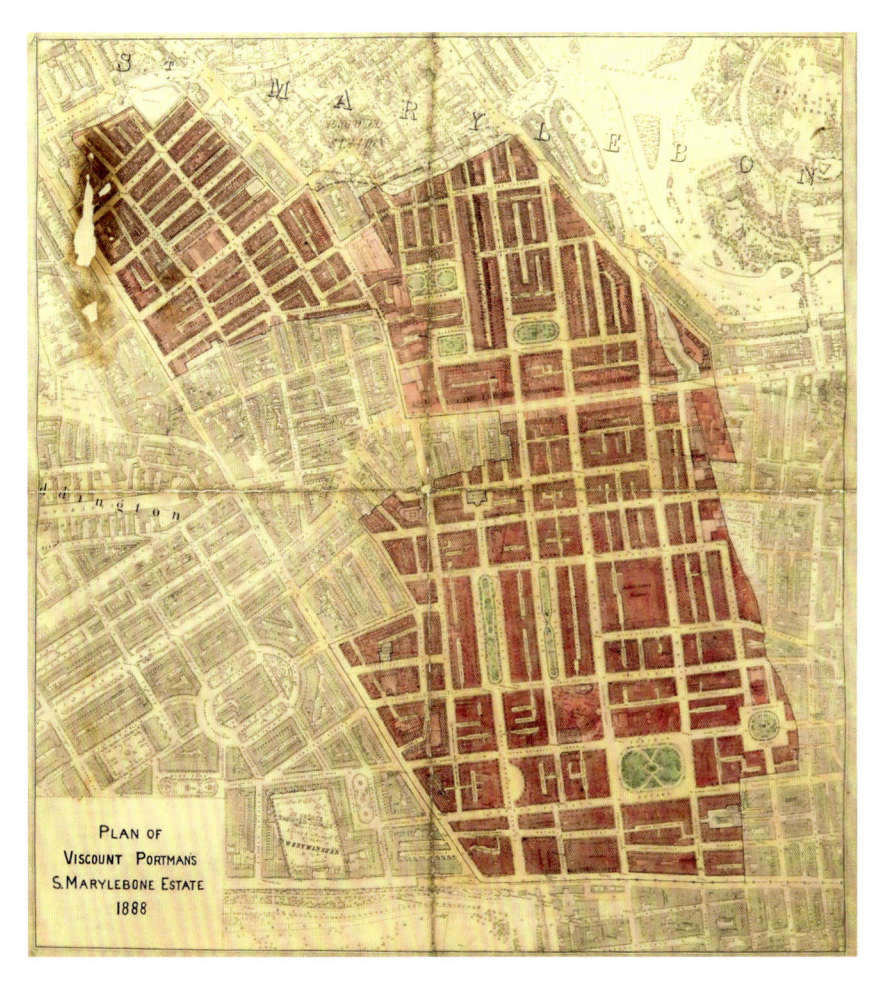

PLAN OF
VISCOUNT PORTMANS
S. MARYLEBONE ESTATE
1888

*The estate at its full extent in 1888, shortly before Marylebone Station was built.*
*Image: The Portman Estate*

and beyond. His best-known work, the Euston Arch of 1837, was demolished in 1961–2 despite the fierce opposition of John Betjeman and many others. In 1885 Frederick Hunt, who led Portman efforts to improve the housing of the poor, was appointed agent on a generous annual salary of £1,200. He had been principal surveyor since 1872 and in 1883–4 was architect of the new Madame Tussaud's building in Marylebone Road. Hunt was a member of the estate's board of trustees until a month before his death in July 1921 – a remarkable total of 49 years – and was remembered as a kindly and respected local figure. He and his wife, who had 12 children, lived for some time in Dorset Square and during Hunt's term as agent a number of very important changes and developments took place as the estate moved into the twentieth century.[9]

Crucially, on Lady Day 1888 many of the London leases came up for renewal. The new rents and entry fines charged as a result generated a huge increase in income, reflected most conspicuously in the rebuilding of Bryanston. The increase was sufficient to attract considerable criticism, some of the most vociferous appearing in a series of articles published in *The Sunday Times*. The author, Frank Banfield, later republished them as a book called *The Great Landlords of London*. In it he claimed that the Portman estate's ground rents went up by a multiple of seven or eight and produced an additional annual income of £1.25 million. Such figures are difficult to confirm or dispute but were generally accepted at the time. Banfield also attacked the Grosvenor and Bedford estates and on the last page of his book included an application form for readers to join the recently-established Leasehold Enfranchisement Association. The leasehold system was coming under scrutiny as never before.

Some of the London tenants, faced with entry fines and increased rents, were able to seek help from the Portman Building Society. This had been formed in 1881 in Chiltern Street as the Portman Chapel Temperance Permanent Benefit Building Society by the minister of the Portman Chapel, the Revd Neville Sherbrooke, and others. Although there was never any direct connection between the estate and the Portman Building Society, its formation was agreed and approved by the

The Residents of Wilcove Place, near Church Street, waiting to thank Lord Portman, July 1915. Two days earlier he had agreed to improvements rather than rebuilding.
*Image:* © *Westminster City Archives*

*A street party in Penfold Street celebrating the end of the First World War, November 1918.
Image:
© Westminster City Archives*

1st Viscount as an encouragement to thrift – and to temperance. Much later it occupied prestigious premises in Portman Square.[10]

The turning-point of 1888 was one impetus for the creation of the estate's characteristic mansion flats. Flats had reached London in the 1850s but had been slow to catch on and had been associated almost from the beginning with philanthropic building for the working classes. By 1890, however, the needs of the growing middle classes, as well as the potential market they represented, resulted in the building of more spacious and comfortable flats. Portman Mansions and York Mansions in Chiltern Street date from this time, as do Bryanston Mansions and York Street Chambers in York Street, the latter for the Ladies' Residential Chambers Company. Montagu Mansions and Bickenhall Mansions followed and by around 1905 two much larger blocks, Cumberland Mansions and, further north, Clarence Gate Mansions, had also been completed. Many of these blocks were developed for the estate by W. H. Scrymgeour and George Dowdney. A number of blocks of mansion flats were also built after the First World War.

Commercial development on the Oxford Street border of the estate also had a major effect at this period. That was particularly true when in 1909 Gordon Selfridge opened his huge Oxford Street department store, filling the so-called 'dead end' of the street. Mayfair's wealthy inhabitants had previously turned right at the top of Bond Street to visit stores such as Marshall & Snelgrove and Peter Robinson. They did so no longer. When Debenham & Freebody, in magnificent new Wigmore Street premises, and two branches of Lyons Corner House near Marble

Arch, were also opened, shoppers were drawn to the west end of Oxford Street as never before.

The estate office changed location on many occasions from the 1830s onwards. Philip Hardwick operated from Cavendish Square before a move to 68 Great Cumberland Place. By the early 1860s the office was in Harewood Place, north of Marylebone Road. Then in 1868 it settled at 27 Upper Baker Street (the former home of Sarah Siddons) which overlooked Regent's Park and was convenient for managing the northern part of the estate. Twenty years later, in 1888, it found a long-term home at 30 York Place (renumbered 111 Baker Street in 1920) and remained there until 1940.

## Famous Names

It was inevitable that the London estate during the nineteenth century became home to many people who made a mark on history. More than 20 blue plaques commemorate them. At various times residents included the great physicist Michael Faraday, the novelists Anthony Trollope, George Eliot and Wilkie Collins, the artist and writer Edward Lear, Britain's first woman doctor, Elizabeth Garrett Anderson, and the mathematician Charles Babbage. He began construction of his 'difference engine', effectively the world's first computer, in a workshop behind his house at 1 Dorset Street during the 1820s. William Pitt the younger lived at 120 Baker Street in 1803–4 and the writer

Baker Street in about 1910. St Paul's Church, built in 1779 as the Portman Chapel, can be seen.
*Image:*
*© Westminster City Archives*

Watercolour of Montagu Mews South, *c.* 1880. Image: © *Westminster City Archives*

and politician Edward Bulwer-Lytton was born at no. 31 in 1803. Among other famous, notorious or remarkable residents were Sake Dean Mahomed, who opened London's first Indian curry house in George Street in 1810, the two south American soldier–statesmen, José de San Martin and Simon Bolivar, the 'prophetess' Joanna Southcott, a group of artists who lived near Lisson Grove in about 1820 including Samuel Palmer, John Linnell and Benjamin Haydon, the dancer and courtesan Lola Montez, who married bigamously at the French Chapel Royal in 1849, the great actress Sarah Siddons, Mary Seacole of Crimean War fame, and E. M. Forster, who was born in 1879 at 6 Melcombe Place.[11]

Sherlock Holmes as depicted in The Strand Magazine, December 1891.
*Image: © Westminster Libraries: Sherlock Holmes Collection, Westminster Reference Library*

In the first half of the nineteenth century there were significant numbers living on the estate who had retired from India and many former slave owners compensated under the 1833 Slavery Abolition Act.[12]

The estate was also home to Alice Keppel, mistress of Edward VII. In 1900 she moved with her husband George from Mayfair to 30 Portman Square and in 1903 took out a 19-year lease. Mrs Keppel was regarded as a very beneficial influence on the king, and people remembered seeing his 'discreet little one-horse brougham', and later his Rolls Royce, waiting outside the house.[13] When the king died in 1910 Mrs Keppel moved back to Mayfair.

But the most famous resident of the London estate was a Victorian detective who never existed at all. He was introduced to the world in 1891 when Sir Arthur Conan Doyle published the first Sherlock Holmes story in the *Strand Magazine*. Thereafter Sherlock Holmes and Dr Watson would be forever linked with their fictional address, 221B Baker Street, the location of which remains a contested mystery. If, as claimed by some, it was on the site of today's no. 31 it has gone for ever, though today's no.109, next to the estate's former office at no.111, gives some idea of what it might have looked like. The real problem is that no. 221, which lies north of Melcombe Street, only came into existence after 1930 when Upper Baker Street was renamed and renumbered. Truth and fiction fail to coincide, but that did not prevent the renaming of York Mews South as Sherlock Mews in 1937, or the placing of a bronze statue of Sherlock Holmes outside Baker Street Station in 1999. For Holmes and Watson immortality is assured.

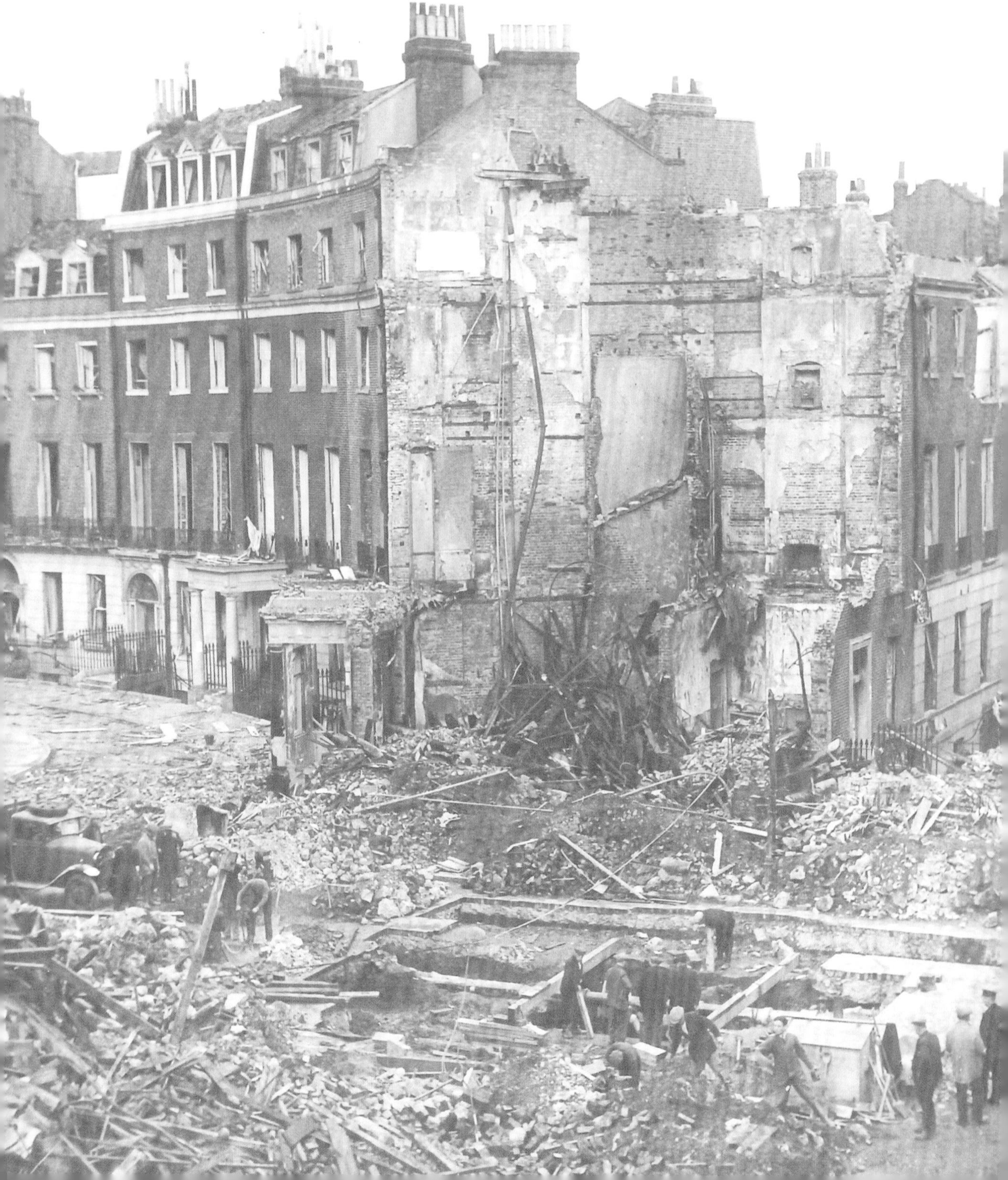

CHAPTER 7

# The Problems Mount

## *Quick Succession*

It had been a major blow for the Portman family when in 1911 the 2nd Viscount's eldest son, Edward (Teddy), died at the age of only 54. He had been playing golf on the hills above Orchard Portman and a chill caught that day turned quickly to double pneumonia. A photograph of his funeral procession, making its way across the Somerset landscape from Hestercombe to Cheddon Fitzpaine, seems to capture a world that was vanishing, not only for the Portmans but for a whole society. Teddy had been groomed to succeed as head of the family and lived in considerable style at Hestercombe. He became a Justice of the Peace, a Deputy Lieutenant of Somerset and a popular local figure. But though he married he never had children and it was his younger brother Henry Berkeley Portman (1860–1923) who succeeded as 3rd Viscount when their father died in 1919.

Henry married Emma Andalusia Frere, widow of the 5th Earl of Portarlington, in 1901. They spent most of their married life at Buxted Park, near Uckfield, East Sussex. It was a fine Palladian mansion and large estate which had descended in Henry's maternal family since the eighteenth century and had once been home of the 3rd Lord Liverpool, Henry's great grandfather. In his father's later years Henry had taken a

The funeral procession of Edward William Berkeley Portman (1856–1911) crosses the estate at Hestercombe on its way to Cheddon Fitzpaine, 1911.
*Image: South West Heritage Trust*

role in managing the London estate by chairing meetings of the board (whose minutes survive in a fine series from 1910 onwards). But his health was fragile and after he inherited he could take no part in public life, looking to his wife, the Viscountess, and his youngest brother, Captain Gerald Portman, for help with estate business. In January 1923 at the age of 62 he died in the mansion at Bryanston, the last of the Portmans to do so, and was buried at Durweston.[1]

Henry left an only daughter, Selina, and on his death the title thus passed to his next surviving brother, Claud Berkeley Portman (1864–1929). In 1887 Claud's grandfather the 1st Viscount had provided for him by buying a 400-acre estate at Child Okeford, near Bryanston, and building him a large country house.[2] It was there in the following year that Claud began his married life with Mary Ada Gordon-Cumming, their daughter Guinevere being born in 1889. But the marriage was far from happy and in 1897 the press was filled with news of divorce proceedings.[3] In 1898 at the British Consulate in Rome, Claud quietly married Harriette Mary Stevenson (herself a divorcee) as his second wife[4] and the same year the eldest of their three children, Edward, was born.

Claud's divorce and remarriage were regarded as scandalous by Victorian society and led to a long-lasting family rift. The 2nd Viscount forbade the family to have any contact with the newly-married couple, and on one occasion he reputedly insisted that his entire party should leave the races at Blandford Forum because Claud and his wife were also present.[5] In June 1906, after reconciliation had proved impossible, Claud decided to leave Dorset altogether, Julietta Forrester recording the occasion in her diary:

> James and I went to Blandford to see Mr & Mrs Claud Portman off for good. Lord P and the family had refused so persistently to countenance the marriage that for the sake of their children they had to sell Child Okeford… They both seemed sad today and he told me that it was 'a very sad leave-taking last Saturday' when he bade adieu for good to Child Okeford. No-one but ourselves were at the station to give them a send-off.[6]

They settled first at Stratford-on-Avon, where Claud won prizes for his shorthorn cattle. Then, after his father's death, he took over from his

Buxted Park, Uckfield, East Sussex, in 1928.
*Image: The Hon. Mrs Rosemary Pease*

brother Henry at Buxted Park and remained there after succeeding to the title in 1923. But in an expression of parental disapproval from beyond the grave, the 2nd Viscount had ensured that Claud gained control only of the entailed estates in Dorset and Somerset. Claud's son, in due course, got only Somerset, though the mistaken assumption of the wider world was that both men derived a vast income from London. This was not the case, control of the London estate having passed in 1923 to the 2nd Viscount's youngest son, Captain Gerald Portman.

Two rapid successions and heavy death duties were real financial shocks to the Portmans. About 7 acres near Church Street, in the northern part of the London estate, were sold in 1919 for £100,000 and in 1921 almost 1,000 acres in the West Country went for £300,000. In 1922 Wentworth Lodge at Boscombe, which had been used as a convalescent home for officers during the First World War, was sold for £28,000, and in 1925 Claud, by now the new Viscount Portman, turned his attention to Bryanston itself. Ignoring protests from the wider family, who never forgave him for what happened next, he decided that the great mansion must be sold. First, in a 14-day auction, the entire contents of the house were disposed of for £34,000 in what one newspaper called 'the sack of Bryanston'. Even the sword which the 6th baronet had taken from the captured Duke of Monmouth was not spared, though some of the portraits remained in family possession. The house itself was finally sold in 1927 for £35,000, and quickly began its new life as Bryanston School. Knighton House and a large Dorset farming estate were retained.[7]

In all the circumstances it is difficult to see what else could have been done. Bryanston required an enormous staff and the family's debts were pressing. Thanks to good management and a greatly increased rental from the London estate the Portmans had weathered the late Victorian agricultural depression. But the introduction of Estate Duty in 1894, and the social and economic changes that followed the First World War, led to

Captain Claud Berkeley Portman (1864–1929), 4th Viscount.
*Image: The Portman Estate*

Aerial view of Bryanston House, *c.* 1980.
Image: Sue Sieger

problems of an entirely different order. It is said that 25% of all land in England changed hands between 1880 and 1930, marking the greatest upheaval in land ownership since the Norman Conquest or the Dissolution of the Monasteries.[8] What happened to the Portmans was only one particularly striking example in a quiet but fundamental social revolution.

## The Somerset Viscount

When Claud died in 1929 he was buried at Cheddon Fitzpaine in Somerset, next to his eldest brother Teddy. Perhaps he felt that even in death Dorset would not have welcomed him. He was succeeded, as 5th Viscount, by his well-liked son, Edward Claud Berkeley Portman (1898–1942), whom his family knew as Eddie and his Somerset tenants as 'Lordy'. He served in the Life Guards during the First World War as one of the Army's youngest lieutenants, and during the Second World War, with the rank of captain, was liaison officer between the Army and

A family group at the Epsom summer meeting in 1921. Left to right: Captain 'Gar' Emmet (facing away), Mrs Emmet, Sylvia G. Portman, Edward Claud Berkeley Portman (later 5th Viscount), Jocelyne Portman (wife of Captain Emmet), and the 4th Viscountess Portman.
*Image: The Hon. Mrs Rosemary Pease*

the Navy during the Plymouth blitz. In 1926 he married Sybil Mary Douglas-Pennant, the youngest daughter of Lord Penrhyn. Together with their two daughters, Sheila and Rosemary, they lived at Staple Fitzpaine Manor, the house which the 1st Viscount had built in about 1840 for his youngest brother the Revd Fitzhardinge Berkeley Portman. A keen sportsman, the 5th Viscount became Master of the Taunton Vale Foxhounds and in 1927 also played a large part in establishing Taunton Racecourse at Orchard Portman. He rarely missed a race meeting there and his colours became known all over the south of England.

He was also an enthusiastic member of the Staple Fitzpaine, Curland and Bickenhall cricket team. Another of its members, Andrew Grabham, remembered a match in which he made 60 runs: 'Lord Portman was so pleased he sent the butler out to the wicket with a drink for me. The butler said, "It won't hurt you", so I drank it. I was out next ball. It was whisky!' A generous landlord and on friendly terms with many of his tenants and employees, he was much mourned when he died in 1942, aged only 44. Two years later, when the Somerset estate was sold to the Commissioners of Crown Lands to pay for Estate Duty, the story of the Portmans in the West Country retreated a little farther into history. A large collection of Portman archives, deposited at the Somerset Record Office in 1940, survives as a record of the family's shaping influence in the county from the fourteenth century onwards.

Until her own death in 1975 the 5th Viscount's widow continued to live at Staple Manor, having bought it from the Crown. She shared in the life of the community and was Master of the Taunton Vale Foxhounds from 1946 to 1951, doing much to re-establish the hunt after the lean years of the war. She was also instrumental in modernising the historic almshouses at Staple Fitzpaine, built by Sir William Portman, the 5th baronet. They flourish today, now managed by a charitable trust, and provide attractive self-contained flats for the elderly.[9]

Because the 5th Viscount left no male heir when he died in 1942, the title now passed back a generation to his uncle, Seymour Berkeley

Sybil Portman and Eddie Portman on voyage from Gibralter to Tangier Sept 1927.
*Image: The Hon. Mrs Rosemary Pease*

Portman (1868–1946), who became 6th Viscount. Aged 74, unmarried and another sick man, he lived at Newlands, a house in Charlton Marshall, near Blandford Forum, and later at Knighton House, Durweston, holding the title for only four years. It then passed down the line once more to the youngest brother, Captain Gerald Berkeley Portman (1875–1948), who, for two years only, was the 7th Viscount.

## Captain Portman

Gerald Berkeley Portman (1875–1948) was a very different character from either his brothers or his nephew. Born in 1875, he joined the 10th Hussars at the age of 20, served in the Boer War and became a captain. In 1901–2 he was aide-de-camp to Lord Curzon, Viceroy of India, and during the First World War served with the 11th and 5th Reserve Field Artillery Regiments. In 1902 he married Dorothy Marie Isolde, the daughter of Sir Robert Sheffield, and moved to Healing Manor, near Grimsby. They had two sons, Gerald and Michael, and it is through Michael that the main line of the Portman family, and the title, have since descended.

Because of the provisions made by the 2nd Viscount, Captain Portman gained control of the London estate in 1923 and retained it until his death 25 years later. He also held the Dorset estate from 1929 and Somerset from 1942 until its sale shortly afterwards. He made his London base at Montagu (or Portman) House (22 Portman Square), but continued to spend a great deal of time at Healing Manor. He also acquired an estate at Inverinate in Scotland, beautifully situated on the

Portrait of Captain Gerald Berkeley Portman (1875–1948), 7th Viscount, by Oswald Birley, 1934.
*Image: The Portman Estate*

*The Problems Mount*  139

Dorothy Isolde, wife of Gerald Berkeley Portman, 7th Viscount.
*Image: The Portman Estate*

shores of Loch Duich near Kyle of Lochalsh. The family often travelled to Scotland in his steam yacht, and a fine set of game books records sporting activities at Inverinate.

Memories of Captain Portman have not always been positive. But he was clearly a decisive and energetic man who presided over the estate during very difficult times. In July 1933 he wrote to his agent, J. H. Furmedge, to express congratulations to Furmedge and his predecessor E. H. Trepplin that after '13 long years of strain and toil' the bill for Estate Duty had finally been settled. The total sum was a vast £2,877,760, paid over 544 weeks at an average of £5,290 a week. 'All that remains now,' Captain Portman added, 'is a Champagne supper!'

Hundreds of letters between Captain Portman and J. H. Furmedge survive in the estate archives for the period 1923 to 1943.[10] Although he lived mainly at Healing or in Scotland he kept in very close touch

Photographs of Gerald Berkeley Portman tiger hunting in Nepal, and with an elephant.
Images: *The Portman Estate*

The 7th Viscount's steam yacht, SY Devonia.
*Image: The Portman Estate*

with the estate, often writing to Furmedge several times a week. Their correspondence provides a fascinating and detailed record of events of many kinds. Captain Portman and his wife clearly enjoyed travelling, and a letter of 1928 from the Esplanada Hotel in San Paolo describes their voyage to Brazil. Then in 1930 they went out to join their daughter, Penelope, in Montreux for Christmas and probably also visited the Captain's sister Mary, the violinist. Mary died in Montreux in January 1931, the Captain arranging for her ashes to be brought home to Durweston to be buried close to the graves of her parents.[11]

## The London Estate Expands

No estate can ever stand still. It needs constant regeneration if it is not to stagnate, and the first half of the twentieth century saw a great many developments on the London estate. There was, of course, considerably more pressure to make a profit than had ever been the case in the previous century.

One of the most conspicuous additions to the area was Marylebone's grandly classical town hall (later Westminster Council House and more recently part of the London Business School). It was completed in 1918 to the designs of Sir Edwin Cooper and extended by him in 1939 to accommodate the public library. It stands in Marylebone Road on a commanding site sold by the estate to St Marylebone Borough Council. The estate's close involvement with housing improvements in Lisson Grove continued after the death of the 2nd Viscount, though for financial reasons it was not possible to repeat his generous death-bed gesture by presenting land to the council for development. The estate did, however, sell off more of its freehold in 'Lissonia', as it was called, and so made possible a number of schemes initiated by London County Council, the St Marylebone Housing Association and the Borough Council. Such schemes gradually transformed the Church Street area and helped it in the slow process of shaking off its reputation for impoverishment. The estate long maintained a link with the St Marylebone Health Society, a charity founded in 1906 to combat child mortality in Lisson Grove and still active until recently. In 1917 Lord Portman provided the Society with a new 'Portman Day Centre' for children, and Captain Portman gave larger premises twenty years later.

Marylebone Town Hall (left) and Portman Mansions (above).
*Both images: The Portman Estate*

The famous 'Roman' interior of the Regal Cinema, Marble Arch, 1928.
*Image: © British Film Institute*

The early years of the twentieth century witnessed other developments of many different kinds. In 1936 the Borough Council built new public baths in Seymour Place, again on land which the estate made available. This was also a golden age for cinemas. The Electric Palace Cinema, one of the earliest in London, opened at 532 Oxford Street, next to Old Quebec Street, in 1908 and three more cinemas opened in the Edgware Road before the First World War (the Connaught, the Blue Hall and the Grand Kinema). In 1928 the famous Regal Cinema opened at Marble Arch (as predecessor of the Odeon) and in 1937 the Classic opened in Baker Street (succeeded in 1973 by the Screen on Baker Street). The estate's film enthusiasts have always been exceptionally well served.

Department stores flourished. In November 1930 Marks and Spencer opened on its present site near Marble Arch, and in the same year the famous boys' outfitters Daniel Neal and Sons, which originated as a bootmaker's in the Edgware Road, moved to premises on the east side of Portman Square. The business remained there for two generations, almost a local institution, until it was sold to John Lewis in 1963. Selfridge's expanded rapidly during the two decades after it first

The Odeon, Marble Arch, and beyond it a Lyon's Corner House restaurant, 1968.
*Image: The Portman Estate*

The Royal Silver Jubilee decorations at Selfridge's, 1937.
*Image: © Selfridges & Co*

opened in 1909, doubling its Oxford Street frontage as well as its floor space and taking over Somerset Street and St Thomas's Church in the process.

Captain Portman must surely have been impressed by what Gordon Selfridge was achieving and by other large-scale developments such as Chiltern Court, the huge block of luxury apartments built above Baker Street Station for the Metropolitan Railway. It was in the context of such major schemes that The Portman Estate made the bold decision to redevelop the east side of Portman Square to create a mansion block called Orchard Court, to be followed shortly afterwards on the square's southern side by Portman Court. Both were completed in 1929 and built in a classical revival style. These radical changes to the appearance of the square happened long before planning permission became a consideration. It is interesting, however, to find a letter from Princess Louise quoted in the board minutes for January 1926 in approval of the Orchard Court scheme. The Princess, who was Queen Victoria's daughter, lived on the north side of Portman Square and her views clearly mattered.[12]

Other mansion flats were being built on the estate throughout this period. They included Bryanston Court in 1927, Harrowby Court, Sherwood Court and Hesketh House in 1928, and Wythburn Court in 1930. By coincidence the amorous meetings of Alice Keppel and Edward VII at 30 Portman Square at the beginning of the century were followed a generation later by those of Wallis Simpson and the Prince of Wales at 5 Bryanston Court. The estate's tendency to attract affairs of this sort had begun in the eighteenth century with the Duke of York and his mistress Mary Ann Clarke, and it was not yet at an end.

Many more mansion blocks followed during the 1930s, including Clarewood Court in 1931, Dudley Court in 1932, Carisbrooke House (15 Portman Square) in 1934 and Stourcliffe Close in 1935. The Mount Royal of 1931 in Oxford Street, was originally built at a cost of over £1 million as 650 serviced flats and is an example of art deco design. The freeholds of the sites of Macready House, built as police flats in Crawford Street in 1922, and of Berkeley Court and Dorset House, two very fine mid-1930s blocks on Marylebone Road, were sold by the estate to developers. Berkeley Court, with its roof garden of more than an acre, was designed by W. E. Masters and Dorset House by T. P. Bennett and Son. At the southern end of Great Cumberland Place, the Cumberland Hotel and the block opposite were deliberately designed to set off the view north from Marble Arch. Together they framed a fine southern approach to the estate in the years when it was beginning to take on its modern appearance.

## The Second World War and After

Development on the estate was cut short by the outbreak of the Second World War. Captain Portman's correspondence with J. H. Furmedge reflects the tension created by the Munich crisis in September 1938 and the build-up to war. Captain Portman even considered moving the London estate office to the country. It was a pity he did not, because the office was bombed twice, first in December 1940 when it was still at 111 Baker Street and again five months later in May 1941, when it had moved to the family's London home, 22 Portman Square. The house was so badly damaged that it had to be demolished. The estate suffered particularly because it was within range of Paddington and Marylebone

Bomb damage at Montagu House, Portman Square, 1941.
*Image: London Metropolitan Archive*

stations, both of which were major targets for German bombers. Well over 1,000 houses on the estate were damaged, many seriously, and there were numerous dramatic losses. Much of the west side of Bryanston Square was destroyed, and there was also serious damage in Great Cumberland Place, around Church Street and in Baker Street. After 22 Portman Square was demolished, the estate office was moved to 12 Portman Square where it remained after the war until it could be moved to the new building at 38 Seymour Street.

Captain Portman had become Master of the Portman Hunt in 1932, and it was thus a bitter blow to him when in 1940 the Government requisitioned the Bryanston horses to be sent abroad. Then, after he had already sold the first of his two yachts, the second was commandeered by the Board of Trade. Game and timber from his various estates in Dorset, Lincolnshire and Scotland were given up, and soon even his staff were being conscripted. 'We are living in a terrible time!', he wrote plaintively in a letter dated 2 September 1939.[13] He moved to the Highlands for many months at a time, taking care to instruct Berry Brothers of St

James's to send most of his wines to Scotland and keeping in close touch with estate affairs.

In London the government requisitioned many estate properties including 64 Baker Street. That became headquarters of the Special Operations Executive (SOE) which also occupied several other addresses nearby. The SOE, whose activities long remained secret, was set up by Churchill in July 1940 after the fall of France, and at its greatest strength had 10,000 men and 3,000 women based in or near the Baker Street

Bomb damage on the west side of Bryanston Square and at the junction of Great Cumberland Place and Seymour Street, 1941.
*Image: The Portman Estate*

HQ. One section was run from a flat in Orchard Court and another was based at 1 Dorset Square from where agents were sent on missions into France. A commemorative plaque was unveiled there in 1957 by the Queen Mother, and another, at 64 Baker Street itself, was unveiled in 2010. SOE agents who were parachuted into Europe practised what some considered to be very un-British techniques such as silent killing with a knife and the use of martial arts. They also engaged in industrial and military sabotage using the recently-developed plastic explosives. The SOE's contribution to the Allied victory was enormous and General Eisenhower reckoned the war was shortened by six months as a result.[14]

Following the death of the 5th Viscount in 1942 it was a relief to Captain Portman when the Commissioners of Crown Lands offered £345,000 for much of the Somerset property. The sale went through two years later, and in November 1946 Captain Portman, having for so long managed the estate, inherited the viscountcy as well on the death of his brother Seymour. In the short time that he held the title two significant events occurred. In April 1947 the estate sold the freehold of its portion of the Selfridge's site, and in 1948 it acquired what is now known as the Portman Burtley Estate in Buckinghamshire.

J. H. Furmedge died in September 1943 and in 1944 he was succeeded as agent by Edward Gillett, then aged 57, who remained in post until 1967. Gillett was a partner of Daniel Smith, Oakley & Garrard, a firm of surveyors which was to have a long association with the estate. Two years after his appointment, when the Institution of Chartered Surveyors acquired its Royal Charter, he became its President and in 1948 he was knighted. The sale of the Selfridge's freehold was made on his advice and agreed by the new Lord Portman because the moment was thought to be right. Selfridge's had been paying £16,000 in annual ground rent, but the sale realised the enormous capital sum of £600,000.

It was decided that half this amount should be invested in agricultural property and by the time Captain Portman died at Healing in September 1948 the trustees had already agreed to buy the Portman Burtley Estate (then known as the Dropmore Estate) for £155,000. Plans to acquire other estates were soon abandoned in view of the looming mountain of Estate Duty. Probate on the 7th Viscount's estate came to £5 million and the total amount of Estate Duty was finally agreed in 1952 at £7.6 million.

It was the 1920s all over again, only this time the impact on the London estate was even more profound. But it is a measure of the estate's resilience that by April 1955 almost the entire amount had been paid, the account finally being closed in December 1956. Initially the possibility of raising money through a loan was considered, but this idea was quickly rejected and more drastic measures were taken instead. In 1950 the remaining 3,800 acres of the Dorset estate were sold to the Crown, realising £120,000. Then in March 1951 and November 1952 the northern part of the London estate was disposed of in two sales. The first sale was of 42 acres north of Marylebone Road, including all the properties in and around Church Street and in Dorset Square, one of the estate's most prized possessions. Even Abbey House, the supposed site of 221B Baker Street, was sold, just at the moment it was to become the setting for the immensely popular Sherlock Holmes Exhibition, St Marylebone's contribution to the Festival of Britain. The second sale was of 41 acres running south from Marylebone Road to Dorset Street. The two sales produced £1.5 million and £1.7 million respectively and ensured that the accounts were in the black again. But the cost had been enormous. The London estate had now been reduced to 110 acres, less than half the 258 acres it contained in 1741.

## The 8th Viscount

On the Captain's death in 1948 the new Lord Portman was his eldest son, Gerald William Berkeley Portman (1903–1967). Gerald was educated at Eton and Sandhurst, joined the Royal Army Service Corps in 1940 and served for most of the war in East Africa, ending it like his father as a captain. Later, again like his father, he became a director of the Alliance Assurance Company. For a time he was on the fringes of Kenya's Happy Valley set, and was even portrayed in the 1988 film *White Mischief*. Immediately after his father's death he began work on forming a new estate company, one of whose aims was to regulate the interests of the tenants for life in order to reduce the liability for death duties. The Portman, London and Dorset Estates Company, which his father had created in December 1941, was wound up and a new Portman, London, Dorset and Buckinghamshire Property Company was incorporated in March 1949. In 1955 it became a business trust, called Portman Family Settled Estates, and was valued at £4 million.

These were years that took their toll. In 1950 Lord Portman presided at the opening of the Old Church Garden in High Street, Marylebone, a project carried out by the newly-formed St Marylebone Society. But he twice declined invitations to speak to the society about the history of the estate owing to the pressure of death duties and the two estate sales, which were heavy blows to him. The creation of the 1955 trust had given

Gerald William Portman, 8th Viscount, and Lady Portman in their Coronation robes, 1953.
*Image: The Portman Estate*

the estate a new status. This new structure meant that Lord Portman did not participate in trust matters and it was the trustees alone who took decisions about how income was to be distributed. Though he now had no managing role, he continued to play a quiet but valued part in local affairs both in London and in Buckinghamshire, where he built a new home, Burtley House.

The 1950s and '60s were extremely active years for redevelopment and were marked by enormous progress for the estate as a whole. There had always been lively hopes for the redevelopment of the bombed out site at 22 Portman Square, but it took some years for plans to come to fruition in the form of the Portman Hotel and the two blocks of flats behind it, Portman Towers. This development had been delayed by the demands of the Town and Country Planning Act 1947, another new hurdle to be faced as the estate adopted a more professional approach to its affairs. These same years also produced, amongst much else, a series of new blocks of flats along Seymour Place and to the north of Bryanston Square, the Jews' College in Montagu Place, the new head offices of Marks and Spencer at 37–67 Baker Street, and the estate's own new office at 38 Seymour Street. The creation of the estate office was part of

29–35 Baker Street, the possible site of Sherlock Holmes's 221B, photographed in 1957.
*Image: The Portman Estate*

a major reconstruction of the east side of Great Cumberland Place, one of the areas that had suffered serious damage during the war. In 1956–7 the first photographic survey of the London estate was carried out. It was followed by later surveys and together they form an invaluable visual record of the estate in a period of recovery and great change.

Throughout the period from the First World War onwards the London estate never lost its distinctive character or its prestige. Portman Square and the streets around it remained some of the most fashionable addresses in the capital and it was no accident that C. P. Snow set his novel *The Conscience of the Rich* in Bryanston Square. The novel, published in 1958, follows the fortunes of a wealthy Anglo-Jewish family during the cultural and political turmoil of the inter-war years.

Though C. P. Snow was not himself a resident of the estate, other writers followed the example of their great Victorian predecessors by making a home there. Early in the century the brilliant author of

*Zuleika Dobson*, Max Beerbohm, lived at 48 Upper Berkeley Street, and the novelist George Gissing lived at various addresses near Baker Street Station. Arnold Bennett and H. G. Wells both lived at Chiltern Court, and Rebecca West at 15 Orchard Court. Rose Macaulay had a flat in St Andrew's Mansions, Dorset Street, before moving to another in Hinde Street, while Somerset Maugham lived in Wyndham Place and later Bryanston Square. One of the greatest literary figures of the twentieth century, T. S. Eliot, spent four years at Crawford Mansions before moving in 1920 to Clarence Gate Mansions, where he remained for twelve years. There he completed *The Waste Land*, published in 1922, the poem which above all others gave a voice to English literary modernism. Eliot's presence locally for so many years, and the poetry he created during that time, provide what are perhaps the most remarkable of all the estate's many literary associations.

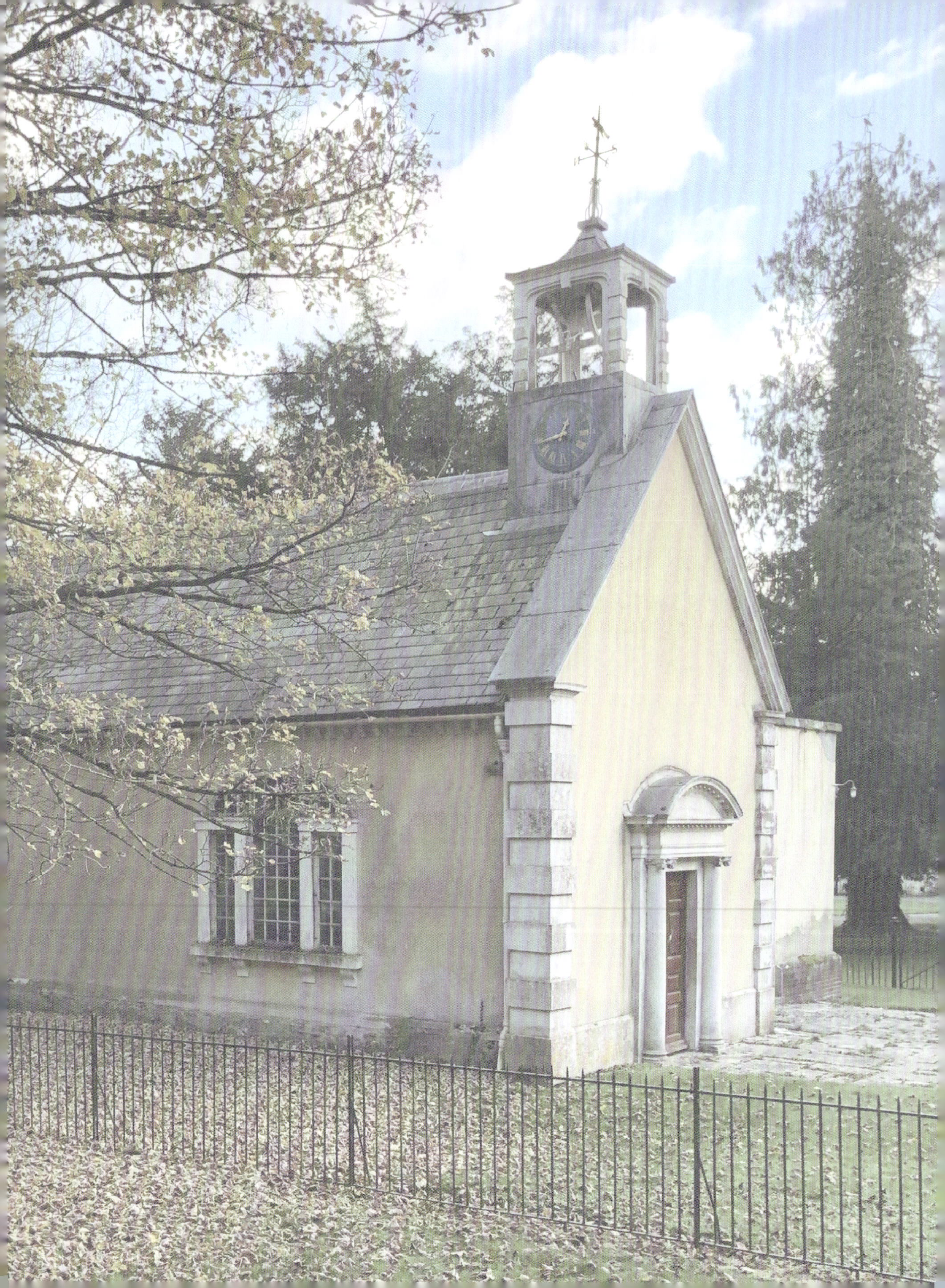

CHAPTER 8

# The Problems Resolved

*A Chapel in the Woods*

Despite the sale of Bryanston in 1927, and of the surrounding estate in 1950,[1] Dorset did not lose its hold on the affections of the Portman family. In September 1945, Michael Berkeley Portman (1906–1959), Captain Gerald Portman's younger son, came to live at Durweston with his second wife Marjorie Kerr Harris. Gerald had offered them Portman Lodge, a comfortable white-painted Georgian house with far-reaching views to the River Stour and to the steep wooded cliff at Bryanston. Close at hand the rambling Knighton House was occupied by Uncle Seymour, the 6th Viscount, who until his death in 1946 lived there 'in solitary state'. Seymour wondered how his nephew would manage in a house as comparatively small as Portman Lodge. But to Michael, Marjorie and the children it seemed like paradise.

Marjorie Portman tried to discover as much as she could about her husband's ancestral territory. Recent family graves lay nearby in the churchyard at Durweston, and in her book *Bryanston: Picture of a Family* she describes how on one longer walk she reached the little Georgian chapel in the woods at Bryanston where so many earlier Portmans are buried. The chapel, standing next to the site of the original mansion, was half derelict and when she forced a way in she found rotting box pews, broken pavements and family memorials reaching back to the

The Portman Chapel today and as it was in 1894 with the former Bryanston House beside it.
*Image: The Portman Estate*

1760s. After the family disruptions of the previous thirty years, this was an important moment of reconnection with the past, and in 1956–7 the chapel was carefully restored. It is now almost the only fragment of the original West Country estate still in Portman ownership.[2]

*Portman family graves in the churchyard at Durweston.*
*Image: The Portman Estate*

Michael Portman served in the Fleet Air Arm and in minesweepers during the Second World War and in 1955 stood unsuccessfully as the Liberal candidate for North Dorset. But then in 1959, at the age of only 53, he died. His brother, the 8th Viscount, survived until 1967, his Viscountess, Nancy Portman, outliving him for 31 years at Sutton Waldron House near Blandford Forum. But because the 8th Viscount had no children it was Michael's elder son by his first marriage, Edward Henry Berkeley Portman (1934–1999), who now succeeded as 9th Viscount.

The new Lord Portman, known to everyone as Eddie, attended the Royal Agricultural College in Cirencester, and began farming at Crowood near Marlborough. Later he moved to Clock Mill, Herefordshire, on the banks of the River Wye, where he bought the nearby Wilmaston Farm, an estate of about 1,000 acres. He was devoted to motor racing and was a gifted musician, playing seven instruments including the clarinet, piano, trumpet and guitar. He was also a reconciler and arranged a party for the entire Portman family at the House of Lords,

*Election flyer for Michael Portman.*
*Image: The Portman Estate*

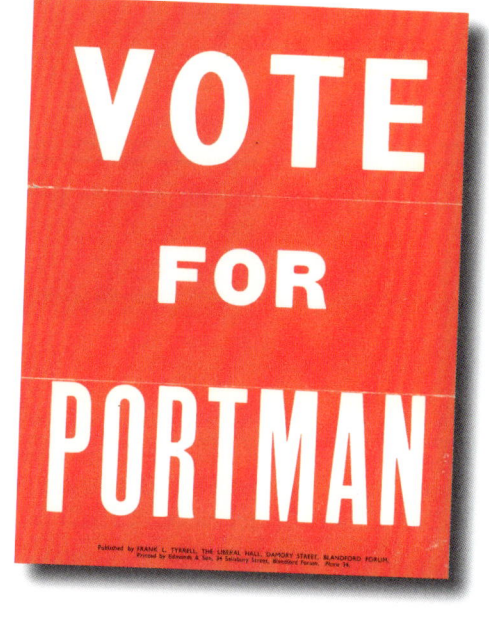

Portrait of Edward Henry Berkeley Portman (Eddie) (1934–1999), 9th Viscount, and Shu Shu, by The Hon. George Bruce, 1989.
*Image: The Portman Estate*

probably the first such gathering of the family since the early days of the century. Like his immediate predecessors, he could have little direct role in the management of The Portman Estate because of the family settlements which placed control in the hands of trustees. The settlement of 1955, which created Portman Family Settled Estates, was followed by a resettlement in 1965 and another in 1976, when a number of new trust funds were established. The estate was now managed in a very different way.

## Winds of Change

The 1950s were a further period of great change for the landscape of London as a new generation of property developers made their fortunes from opportunities provided by the war-damaged city. London's old family estates, used to more conservative methods, sometimes struggled to keep up, having long valued stewardship above profit. But London was now dominated by commercial pressures that were often difficult to challenge or control.[3]

The pace on The Portman Estate quickened in the later 1950s under the leadership of Sir Edward Gillett, its long-serving agent. He was also adviser to the Church Commissioners and the Crown Estate, and believed that a careful alliance with commercial interests now offered a way forward.

In 1957, a new headquarters for Marks and Spencer, Michael House, was completed in Baker Street.[4] Then, in 1962–4, two new seven-storey blocks were built on the south side of Portman Square (nos 39–42).[5] They were part of a transformation of the Square which had begun in 1929 with the building of Orchard Court and Portman Court. It continued in the later 1960s when the bombed-out site at 22 Portman Square was at last redeveloped as the setting for the Portman Hotel and the two Portman Towers, and finally in 1970 when the Churchill Hotel was completed on the square's western side. At this time the estate was working partly in cooperation with the developer Max Rayne (later Lord Rayne).

The extent of new development inevitably attracted criticism, but an internal report on the years 1955–67 defended the estate's approach:

> A special problem was encountered in some redevelopment schemes, arising out of the historical character and associations of the original buildings… Faced with the insuperable problem of adapting the Georgian façades at an economic cost to multi-purpose buildings with interiors related to present day needs in streets and squares where residential demands have fallen, some sacrifices to antiquity were inevitable. The changed need for commercial and office buildings… resulted generally

in the replacement (particularly in Portman Square and Baker Street, but also elsewhere) of buildings in the modern style, although generally of pleasing appearance.

The estate's decisions were subject to increasingly complex planning legislation. The gardens in Bryanston, Montagu, Portman and Manchester squares were already protected under the London Squares Preservation Act of 1931. But the introduction by the post-war Labour government of The Town and Country Planning Act 1947, which established the concepts of planning permission and listed buildings, was a comprehensive attempt to manage development in the built environment. Equally important were the powers given to local authorities to declare Conservation Areas under the Civic Amenities Act 1967. In the Act's first year Westminster City Council, which succeeded St Marylebone Borough Council in 1965, designated much of The Portman Estate as a Conservation Area, extending it in 1979 and again in 1990. By 2003 the Conservation Area contained about 675 Listed Buildings described within 129 listings. They included complete Georgian terraces, the great Home House at 20 Portman Square ('immaculately restored' for use as a private club in 1996–9), five places of worship, five pubs, and the drinking fountain outside Hertford House.[6]

The estate during the 1960s and later was destined to be associated with some of the stories that defined a generation. In 1963 John Profumo, Harold Macmillan's Secretary of State for War, resigned after having an affair with Christine Keeler, an aspiring model with links to a Soviet spy. The world was fascinated, eagerly reading about Profumo, Keeler and Mandy Rice-Davies as well as of events at 17 Wimpole Mews and 1 Bryanston Mews West.[7]

Four years after the Profumo affair the Beatles opened their Apple shop at 94 Baker Street and divided local opinion when they covered it with a psychedelic mural. In the end it was left to the estate to solve the problem. Although the building was no longer Portman property the mural, the estate pointed out, infringed a covenant in the original lease. The Beatles were also establishing other local links at this time. Their main recording studio was at EMI House in Manchester Square, and a flat at 34 Montagu Square, later marked with a blue plaque, was successively the home of Ringo Starr, Paul McCartney and John Lennon. It was there in October 1968 that Lennon was arrested for possessing cannabis, admitting the offence at Marylebone Magistrates Court the following month.[8]

In 1979 a scandal greater even than the Profumo affair was revealed by Margaret Thatcher. She announced to the House of Commons

*The Beatles' Apple shop, 94 Baker Street, 1967. Image: © Rex Features*

that Sir Anthony Blunt, former director of the Courtauld Institute at 20 Portman Square, and Surveyor of the Queen's Pictures, had been a Soviet spy both before and during the Second World War. MI5 had known this since 1964 but gave him immunity in exchange for a full confession. For that reason he was able to remain in post at Portman Square, where he had a flat, until his retirement in 1974. Stripped of his knighthood and his reputation, Blunt died of a heart attack in 1983 at his final home in Portsea Place, just west of the estate.[9]

## *New Ideas*

Sir Edward Gillett finally retired in 1967, having served as agent of the estate during 23 eventful years. His successor Tony Brock, in post until 1989, played a significant role in the rearrangement of the trusts in 1976, creating a trust structure which remains broadly in place to this day. Tony Brock remained as a trustee until the end of 1999.

Charles Hatherell, who guided the estate during the 1990s, in turn brought continuity through his long service as did Frank Gibson, Estate Secretary from 1964 to 1990. In the 1970s Berkeley Portman, a cousin of the 9th Viscount, was Chairman of Trustees, and was succeeded in 1980 by Sir Evelyn de Rothschild. Lord Goodman, who had been a friend of Michael Portman's, was also closely involved as a trustee and as chairman of several Portman family trusts. In 1993 a lawsuit was brought against him alleging misuse of trust funds. The case was only settled in 1999, four years after Lord Goodman's death.[10]

On 2 May 1999 the 9th Viscount himself died at the age of 65 and was succeeded by his son Christopher Edward Berkeley Portman (b. 1958) as 10th Viscount. Christopher Portman rapidly decided that the London estate needed rejuvenation and from the first, as a Director of Portman Settled Estates Limited, took a more active role in estate business than his immediate predecessors. Richard Lay, like Sir Edward Gillett a former President of the Royal Institution of Chartered Surveyors, became Chairman of Trustees and Hugh Seaborn, who had previously worked for Richard Ellis Limited (later known as CBRE), was appointed to the new post of Chief Executive. Under a restructured staff, and with a Board of Directors chaired by Lord Portman, the estate embarked on a major programme of refurbishment and innovation. When Gareth Clutton became Chief Executive in 2008 the task of creating a more modern and responsive organisation continued. He quickly won the affection and respect of his colleagues and was responsible for the much needed move to larger and more up-to-date office accommodation at 40 Portman Square, a new nine-storey building in Portland stone and glass. The move duly took place in November 2011 but without Gareth Clutton to guide it. He had died six months earlier at the age of only 51[11] and was succeeded by Bill Moore, then recently retired from a distinguished army career. The estate is now led by Oliver Fenn-Smith who was previously the Property Director and who, together with the trustees, under John Wythe's chairmanship, runs a modern estate office with around 75 employees.

The 110 acres of the present-day estate are divided equally between residential property, office accommodation and retail premises. There are over 700 rented flats, 150 shops and restaurants, and 32 hotels, of which the Hard Rock Hotel (formerly the Cumberland), with a thousand beds, is the largest. Between 2001 and 2016 over 450 properties were either refurbished or redeveloped, notable schemes including the Gloucester Place regeneration, completed in 2013. A major initiative was the launch in 2001 of Portman Village. Now

Portrait of Christopher Edward Berkeley, 10th Viscount Portman, by David Cobley, 2010.
*Image: The Portman Estate*

rechristened Portman Marylebone, it successfully established New Quebec Street and Seymour Place as a retail quarter managed by the estate and largely occupied by independent retailers. The concept was extended in 2009 when the estate took over management of retailing in Chiltern Street, also part of Portman Marylebone. As a result there are more, and more varied, opportunities for shopping and dining than ever before in the estate's recent history: Condé Nast even called Chiltern Street 'London's coolest street'. The environment has also benefited as schemes which favour pedestrians over cars have been put in place. They include a public realm scheme completed for Portman Square in January 2012.[12]

In 2016 the estate announced further ambitious plans founded on major investment over six years. Schemes would include everything from the careful regeneration of historic streetscapes and the redevelopment of key sites to the creation of new low-energy eco-homes. In addition, working with the Baker Street Quarter Partnership, as well as with local authorities and others, the estate aims to recover a sense of neighbourhood for Baker Street and Gloucester Place. Instead of a traffic-choked one-way highway, it now forms a 'two-way boulevard that is more pedestrian and cycle friendly, with wider pavements and welcoming street-level shops and restaurants'.[13] After many years of planning, the new traffic scheme finally opened in February 2019.

## Beyond London

In 2003 an unexpected acquisition was made. The old Portman town house in Taunton, at 15 Fore Street, came on the market and was bought by the trustees in recognition of the family's long connection with Somerset. This fine medieval building had been owned by the Portmans until 1824 and was now gathered into the estate once more. It is leased as a popular coffee shop.

The composition of the English rural estate has remained largely unchanged during the last 40 years. The Scottish estate at Inverinate, where Captain Gerald Portman spent so much time, was finally sold in 1980, but since the death of the 9th Viscount the large farming estate at Wilmaston, near Hereford, has continued to be managed for the Portman family. The farm is notable not only for being self-sustaining in its energy requirements but also for its innovative water and woodland conservation programmes.

Burtley House in Buckinghamshire was sold following the death of the 8th Viscount in 1967. But the surrounding estate, now called the Portman Burtley Estate, has become the setting for one of the family's most important enterprises outside London. The estate consists of about 1,000 acres of grazing and a similar amount of mixed woodland lying between Hedgerley, Farnham Common and Beaconsfield. It is farmed organically and is chiefly devoted to beef production, a prize-winning herd of 200 pedigree South Devon cattle grazing pasture on which no artificial fertilizers are used. Customers for Burtley beef include Waitrose and the Churchill Hotel in Portman Square. The Burtley woodlands contain several fine beech stands as well as high-quality pine, larch and fir plantations. At Burtley the Portman family are proving themselves the same careful stewards of the natural environment that their ancestors so often sought to be in previous generations.

*****

1–9 Seymour Street, built in 2018.
Image: The Portman Estate

There was a time after the Second World War when the future seemed bleak for London's great private estates. In the last seventy years The Portman Estate has faced estate duty, leasehold reform, new planning legislation and an often uncertain economic climate. But an adaptability and resilience acquired over the centuries has ensured not only that the estate has survived but that it thrives today in the rapidly changing circumstances of the early twenty-first century. The estate has been able to invest in regeneration and new ideas, taking forward a contemporary estate within an historic context. It has also turned more of its attention to its traditional role as a support to the community and an advocate for Marylebone.

Through a Corporate Responsibility Strategy the estate seeks, among many other things, to care for the environment, to enhance local employment opportunities and to provide targeted support for key areas of community need. Grants and donations from The Portman Foundation have in recent years funded many projects in Marylebone and the surrounding area. They range from initiatives to support the West London Mission and its work with the homeless to projects to provide opportunities and facilities for young people and local schools.

The Portman family's journey from provincial Somerset and Dorset to the heart of the capital has been long, complex and always challenging. But an ability over many generations to identify opportunity and to use it wisely built the strong foundations for long-term success. Almost 500 years after Sir William Portman first acquired his lease of lands in the fields of Marylebone, the Portman family's remarkable story of achievement is not nearly at an end.

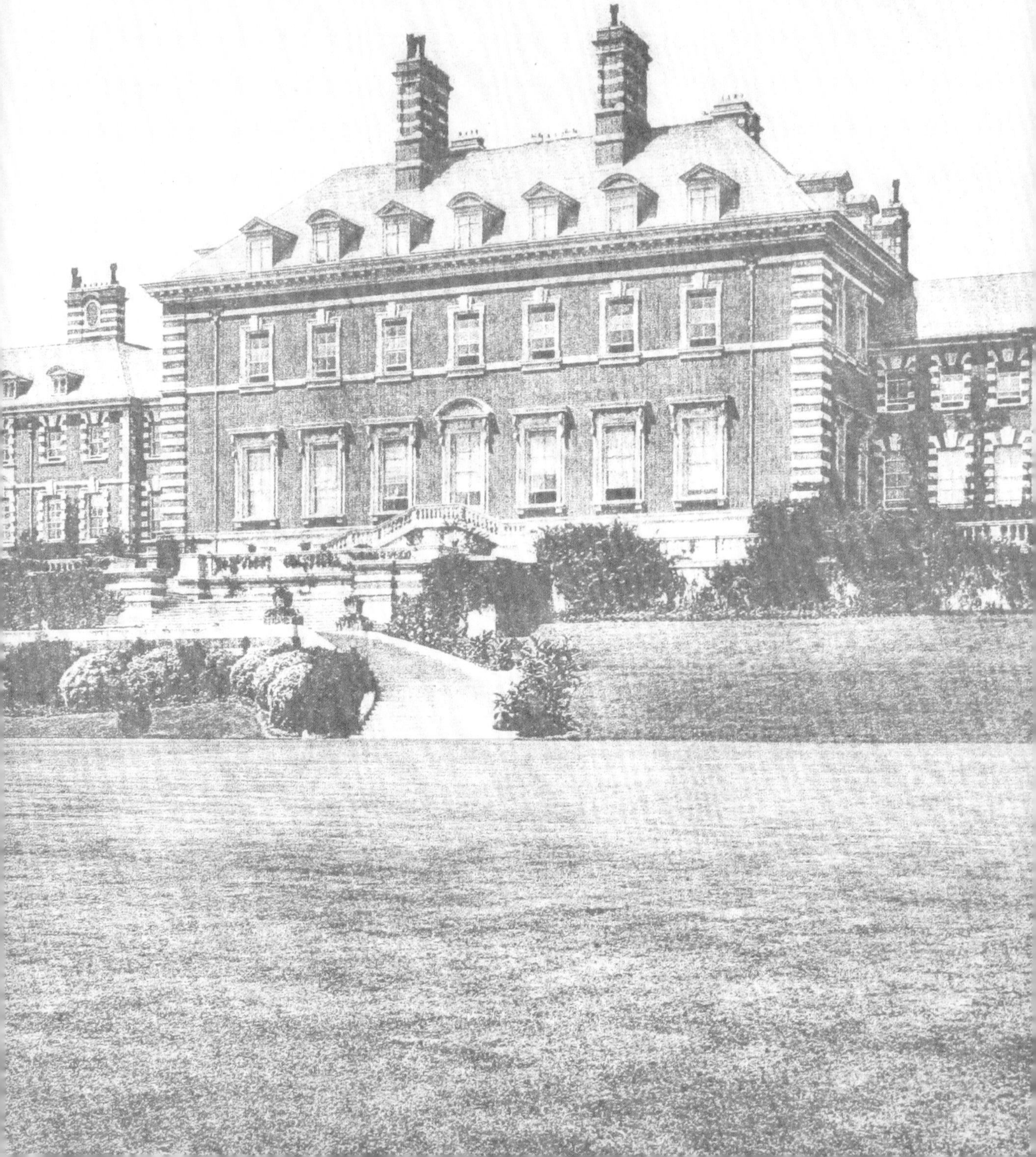

# Appendix

*Letter of Richard Norman Shaw to William Henry Berkeley Portman, 2nd Viscount Portman, 28 March 1889*

29, Bloomsbury Square,
London, W.C.
March 28th, 1889

My Lord,

I am sending you 3 sketch plans for rebuilding Bryanston House on the site we looked at. The more I think of it, the more I feel that in style we ought to adhere to the style of the existing house. I daresay you will laugh and recall to mind my talk about mullioned windows &c. but that was in the first blush and before I had time to really reflect over the subject. Were there nothing else, there is the question of sentiment! You have always been used, for more than a Century to have your family house of that character – and one should not think too lightly of that especially as it is of such a very good & dignified character. But then there is the important question of using up as much of the old house as possible, such as *all* doors, chimney pieces &c. & to make a satisfactory result we must adhere to the style.

In the plans themselves I have tried to embody all your requirements, and I hope you will say they come in fairly well. Of course they require a great deal more working out – good plans are only done after much study – there are so many little refinements which give finish to a work which are not to be done straight off – but these plans are I hope quite matured enough to begin to talk over.

You will see that I am attempting a strictly regular house free from all the irregularities & eccentricities which mar much modern work – in a house of this kind you don't want them – the house should be simple & dignified & it should hold its own on these lines. I have also tried to keep it compact as in a large house the offices are so apt to straggle away, covering a great deal of ground, often in rather an unsightly way.

If I remember right, the ground falls a good deal towards the East, and this I should propose to utilize by getting a basement over one wing and sinking the kitchen court a little. This would give us excellent office space without spreading over much area. The kitchen, scullery & Servants Hall, I should keep very high, so as to have ample air space, and these places would mostly look East, so as to have the morning sun. In connexion with the kitchen we should have an ample range of Larders of moderate height, say 10 feet, with Housekeepers & women servants rooms over. You will think I am devoting too much attention to the offices, but the rest of the plans speak for themselves, and I feel that you will understand them all at a glance, as there are no complications of any sort. I cannot help feeling that we are a little overdone at the existing House by the number & especially the size of the rooms on the top floor. Some of them are so *very* large, about 26 feet square I sh$^d$ think. Would it at all meet your views to make the main part of the new house two stories only – a lofty ground floor, and of course good high rooms for the principal Bed rooms, and for the top floor have rooms with good dormers. I don't mean regular attics, but perhaps not quite square rooms. This avoids making the house so high and we get the rooms somewhat reduced in size – thus a room that on the principal bed room floor would be 26 feet square, would on the next floor not be more than 20.

This, I feel, is rather a detail, but it occurred to me so I thought I might mention it. The important question is whether the general scheme of house I now send meets your views at all. If so, we shall soon get all the minor points adjusted.

Believe me I remain
My Lord, yours faithfully
R. Norman Shaw

The Right Honourable
The Viscount Portman

[Portman Estate Archives, ref. P/F3/113/1. Punctuation slightly regularised.]

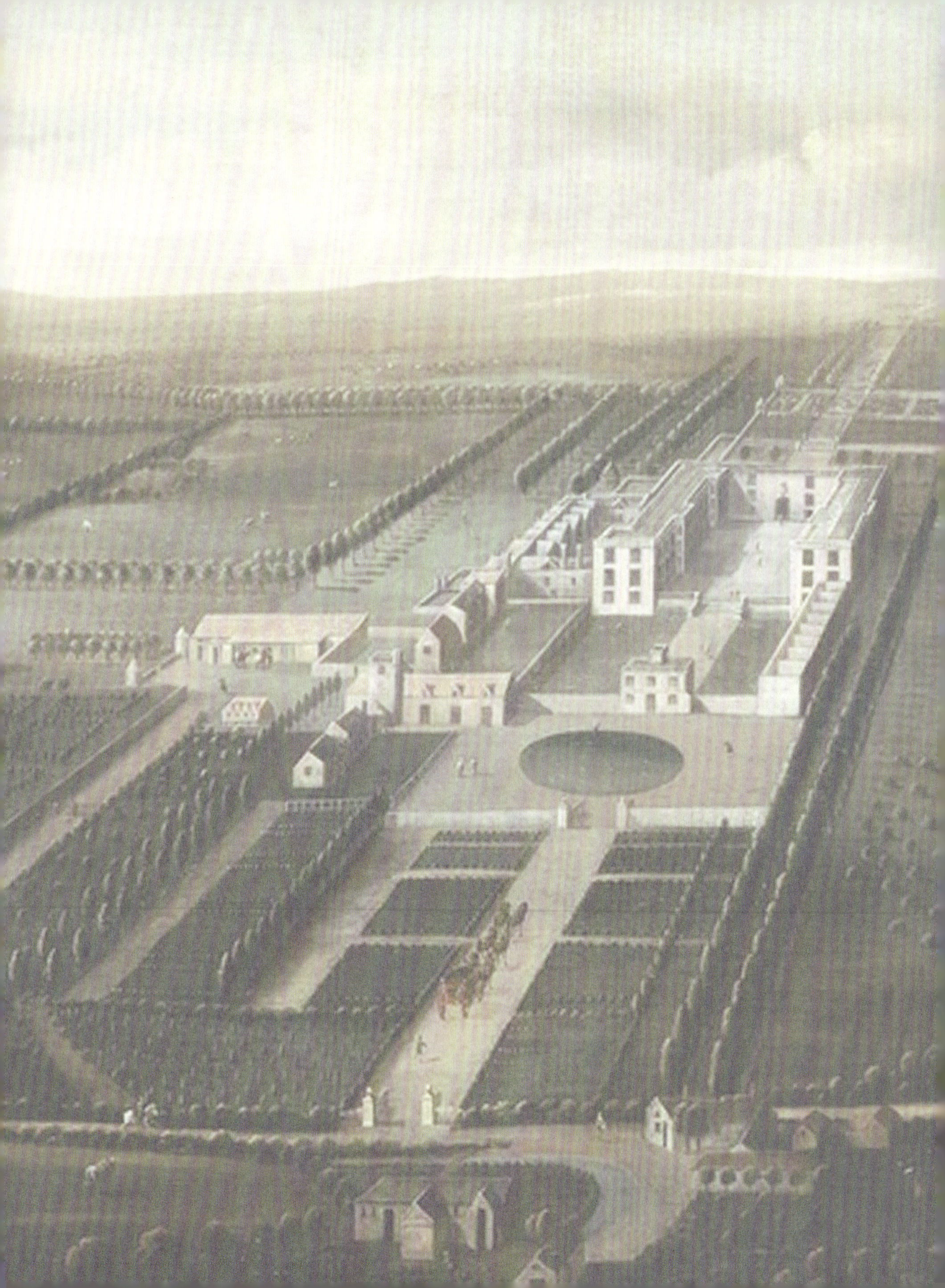

# Notes and References

**Abbreviations Used**

| | |
|---|---|
| Archives | Portman Estate Archives, London |
| Bateman | John Bateman, *The Great Landowners of Great Britain and Ireland* (4th ed., 1883) |
| BL | The British Library, London |
| *CSPD* | *Calendar of State Papers Domestic* |
| *ODNB* | *Oxford Dictionary of National Biography* |
| Forrester | Diary of Julietta Forrester, 1856–1917 (unpublished) |
| Green | Emanuel Green, *The March of William of Orange through Somerset* (1892) |
| Hawkins | M. J. Hawkins, 'Wardship, Royalist Deliquency and Too Many Children: The Portmans in the Seventeenth Century', *Southern History*, vol. 4 (1982), pp 55–89 |
| Henning | B. D. Henning, *The History of Parliament: The House of Commons, 1660–1690* (1983) |
| HRO | Hampshire Record Office, Winchester |
| Hutchins | John Hutchins, *The History and Antiquities of the County of Dorset* (3rd ed., 1861–70) |
| Mayberry | T. W. Mayberry, *Orchard and the Portmans* (1986) |
| Moore | S. T. Moore, *History of Bryanston, Part One, The Narrative* (unpublished report for Bryanston School, 1993) |
| Nathan | Sir Matthew Nathan, *The Annals of West Coker* (1957) |
| Portman | Marjorie Portman, *Bryanston: Picture of a Family* (1987) |

| | |
|---|---|
| Roberts | George Roberts, *The Life, Progresses, and Rebellion of James, Duke of Monmouth* (1844) |
| Saint | Andrew Saint, *Richard Norman Shaw* (1976) |
| SHC | Somerset Heritage Centre, Taunton |
| Smith | Thomas Smith, *A Topographical and Historical Account of the Parish of St Mary-le-bone* (2 editions, both 1833) |
| TNA | The National Archives, Kew |
| Vivian-Neal | A. W. Vivian-Neal, 'Materials for the History of Orchard Portman', *Proceedings of the Somerset Archaeological and Natural History Society*, vol. 89 (1944), pp. 35–53 |
| Walford | Edward Walford, *Old and New London* (1878) |
| WCA | Westminster City Archives, London |

**Chapter 1: Origins**

1. Tom Mayberry, *The Vale of Taunton Past* (1998), chapters 1 and 2.
2. P. H. Reaney, *A Dictionary of British Surnames* (1976, ed.), p. 279.
3. Hawkins, p. 57; HRO, refs 11M59/B1/63 and 11M59/B1/64; R. J. E. Bush, 'The Tudor Tavern, Fore Street, Taunton', *Proceedings of the Somerset Archaeological and Natural History Society*, vol. 119 (1974–5), pp 15–21.
4. J. S. Roskell, Linda Clark and Carole Rawcliffe, *The History of Parliament: The House of Commons 1386–1421*, vol. 4 (1992), pp 122–4.
5. Vivian-Neal, pp 35–53; SHC, ref. DD/PM 5/2/14.
6. S. T. Bindoff, *The History of Parliament: The House of Commons 1509–1558*, vol. 3 (1982), pp. 139–40; Hawkins, pp. 59–60; Vivian-Neal, p. 47; Smith, pp. 38–9.
7. The Revd F. W. Weaver, *Somerset Medieval Wills 1531–1558*, Somerset Record Society, vol. 21 (1905), p. 188; J. G. Nichols (ed.), *The Diary of Henry Machyn Citizen and Merchant-Taylor of London (1550–1563)*, Camden Society, vol. 42 (1848), pp. 125–6; for the possibility that Sir William's heart was buried at Orchard Portman *see* Vivian-Neal, p. 47, n. 59.
8. HRO, ref. 11M59/B1/100.
9. Leonard Knyff's painting is in the Royal Collection, ref. RCIN 406743; James Blackamore's drawings are held by Somerset County Museums Service (South West Heritage Trust, Taunton); *Somerset and Dorset Notes and Queries*, vol. 13 (1913), pp. 320–5.
10. Hawkins, pp 60–2; *Victoria County History of Surrey*, vol. 3 (1911), pp. 482–7; Nikolaus Pevsner, *The Buildings of England: South and West Somerset* (1958), p. 338; *Victoria County History of Somerset*, vol. 3 (1974), p. 41; Bateman, p. 365.
11. Vivian-Neal, p. 49; for pedigrees of the Portman family *see* Hutchins, vol. 1, pp. 254–6, and Mayberry, pp. 50–2; Bridget Cherry and Nikolaus Pevsner, *The Buildings of England: Devon* (2nd ed., 1989), pp. 486–90.
12. *An Inventory of the Historical Monuments in the City of Oxford* (The Royal Commission on Historical Monuments of England, 1939), pp. 118–23.

13 T. G. Barnes, *Somerset 1625–1640* (1961), p. 207, n. 5; *Victoria County History of Somerset*, vol. 2 (1911), p. 206.

14 C. E. H. Chadwyck-Healey, *Hopton's Narrative*, Somerset Record Society, vol. 18 (1902), p. 47; R. G. Hedworth Whitty, *The History of Taunton under the Tudors and Stuarts* (unpublished PhD thesis, University of London, 1938), p. 59.

15 TNA, ref. C10/29/49, being depositions, etc., in the Chancery case Grace Portman v. Richard Batt, 1652.

16 Emanuel Green, 'The Siege and Defence of Taunton, 1644–5', *Proceedings of the Somerset Archaeological and Natural History Society*, vol. 25 (1879), p. 34; BL, Thomason Tracts, E281(25); Historical Manuscripts Commission, *13th Report*, appendix, pt 1, vol. 1, p. 197.

17 SHC, ref. D/P/orch. p. 2/1/1; Richard Batt states (TNA, ref. C10/29/49) that Sir William, a prisoner during the second siege, borrowed £40 from Anthony Mudford, a butcher then serving as a soldier for Robert Blake. This was evidently the same £40 mentioned in the *Calendar of the Proceedings of the Committee for Compounding*, p. 614. That Sir William was a prisoner in Taunton is also mentioned in the *Journal of the House of Commons*, vol. 4, p. 45. He was presumably taken prisoner at the beginning of the second siege since he was still able to grant property in East Chinnock on 3 December 1644 (mentioned in TNA, ref. C10/467/26).

18 BL, Thomason Tracts, ref. E260 (25) and (33), E284 (8), E292 (1) and (21).

19 Nathan, pp. 285 and 290; *Journal of the House of Commons*, vol. 4, p. 178 and 276; Vivian-Neal, p. 50; *CSPD 1661–2*, p. 63; SHC, ref. D/P/orch. p. 2/1/1.

20 TNA, ref. C10/29/49; Nathan, p. 292; *Proceedings of the Somerset Archaeological and Natural History Society*, vol. 99 (1944), p. 15; R. A. Sixsmith, *Staple Fitzpaine and the Forest of Neroche* (1958), p. 45.

**Chapter 2: Heirs and Successors**

1 Hawkins, pp. 72–4; *Journal of the House of Commons*, vol. 5, p. 592; *CSPD, 1661–1662*, p. 63; Nathan, pp 309–10; Moore, p. 95.

2 *Publications of the Harleian Society*, vol. 8 (1873), p. 8; Henning, vol. 3, pp 265–7; Vivian-Neal, p. 51; Thomas Axe refers to Hooke and Halley in his will as 'my good friends' (TNA, ref. PROB 11/406); E. S. Beer (ed.), *The Diary of John Evelyn*, vol. 4 (1955), p. 206 (the 'Portman' referred to in Pepys's diary is one John Poortmans, not Sir William Portman).

3 James Savage, *The History of Taunton* (1822), pp. 250 and 256; *CSPD, 1680–1681*, p. 515.

4 SHC, ref. D/P/orch. p. 2/1/1; *CSPD, 1683*, p. 338; Henning, vol. 3, p. 266; A. B. Connor, *Monumental Brasses in Somerset* (1970, ed.), pp. 130–1; SHC, ref. Q/SR 158/18.

5 For Hugh Speke *see ODNB*, and cf. *CSPD, 1677–1678*, p. 420, and *CSPD, 1679–1680*, pp. 206–7 and 505; for Sir Edward Seymour *see ODNB*; *CSPD,*

*1683* contains several letters of Sir Edward Seymour dated from Orchard Portman.

6 *CSPD, 1664–1665*, p. 476; Richard Baxter, *An Account of the Life and Death of… Joseph Alleine* (2nd ed., 1815), pp 90–1; *CSPD, 1661–1662*, p. 63.

7 *CSPD, 1 July–30 September 1683*, p. 290; *CSPD, 1679–1680*, p. 570.

8 *CSPD, 1679–1680*, p. 20; *CSPD, 1680–1681*, p. 515; *CSPD, 1 July–30 September 1683, passim*.

9 This account of the early stages of the rebellion is based almost exclusively on the papers of 'Mr Axe' (BL, Harleian Ms 6,845, ff. 284–288v); the Thynne papers (Longleat House), vol. 22, f. 172v, refer to Sir William Portman's presence in Lyme Regis.

10 *CSPD, 1 January–30 June 1683*, p. 322; Thynne papers (Longleat House), vol. 22, f. 172v; Historical Manuscripts Commission, *Report on the Manuscripts of Mrs Stopford-Sackville*, vol. 1 (1904), p. 15.

11 The account of Monmouth's flight and capture is based on *An Account of the Manner of Taking the Late Duke of Monmouth* (London, 1685), *A True and Perfect Account of the Taking of James Late Duke of Monmouth* (Dublin, 1685) and T. B. Macaulay, *The History of England from the Accession of James the Second* (1848).

12 Roberts, vol. 2, p. 223; Hutchins, vol. 3, p. 506.

13 *Appendix to the Seventh Report of the Royal Commission on Historical Manuscripts* (1879), p. 417; Green, pp 57–8.

14 Green, p. 64; BL, ref. Add. Ms 32,095, ff. 300–1; Churchill College, Cambridge, ref. Erle-Drax Ms 2/50.

15 SHC, ref. DD/SF 13/2/10; the witnesses to Sir William Portman's first will include Thomas Millington and Richard Lower (SHC, ref. DD/PM 1/6/9).

16 Sir William Portman's illness and death are recounted in Moore, pp 101–7 (based on the legal case in TNA, ref. C22/738/2).

17 Humphrey Sydenham, *The Royall Passing-Bell: or Davids Summons to the Grave. A Sermon preached (lately) in the Parish-Church of Orchard-Portman in Somerset. At the Funerall of the most hopefull, and truly-noble, Sir Hugh Portman* (London, 1630); SHC, ref. DD/PM 1/6/9 and 1/6/10 (first and second wills of Sir William Portman).

18 Eveline Cruickshanks, Stuart Handley and D. W. Hayton, *The History of Parliament: the House of Commons 1690–1715* (2002), vol. 5, pp. 443–4; the portrait of Henry Seymour Portman is in the Yale Centre for British Art, Paul Mellon Collection; the portrait of Meliora Fitch was sold from a private collection at Sotheby's, New York, 27 May 2004.

19 Surviving letters of Henry Seymour Portman to Lord Hatton, 1690–1700 (BL, ref. Add. Ms 29,569, ff. 273–312) are almost all dated from London, Bryanston or Bath, and only two from Orchard Portman; Royal Commission on Historical Monuments (England), *An Inventory of the Historical Monuments in Dorset*, vol. 1 (1952), pp. 217–8 (listed as 'Lord Digby's School'); SHC, ref. D/P/orch. p. 2/1/2.

20 TNA, ref. PROB 11/622.
21 Hutchins, vol. 1, pp. 255 and 262.
22 Romney Sedgwick, *The History of Parliament: the House of Commons 1715–1754* (1970), vol. 2, p. 362; *London Evening Post*, January 1761.
23 Hugh Belsey, 'Gainsborough, Thomas (1727–1788)', *ODNB* (2004).
24 *London Evening Post*, October 1738.
25 Hutchins, vol.1, p. 251; *Somerset and Dorset Notes and Queries*, vol. 13 (1913), pp. 320–5; Leonard Knyff's painting is in the Royal Collection, ref. RCIN 406633.
26 The map of Bryanston, 1659, by William and Margaret Bowles, was sold at Sotheby's, London, 9 December 2014.
27 D. M. Low, *Gibbon's Journal to January 28th, 1763* (1929), pp. 77–8.
28 Moore, pp. 123–4; Anne Hosford, *The Bulbarrow Turnpike and the Portmans* (Dorset County Museum, unpublished essay, revised 1991).
29 Orchard House was standing in March 1842 when furniture was auctioned there (*Taunton Courier*, 2 March 1842), but had been demolished by November 1844 (Roberts, vol. 2, p. 314).
30 For James Wyatt *see ODNB*; for the Wyatt mansion *see* Hutchins, vol. 1, p. 263; for a plan of the ground floor see Archives, ref. P/F 8/69, and Portman, unnumbered plate.
31 The gatehouse and other structures pre-dating the Norman Shaw mansion at Bryanston are described in John Newman and Nikolaus Pevsner, *The Buildings of England: Dorset* (1972), pp. 118–21, and Royal Commission on Historical Monuments (England), *An Inventory of Historical Monuments in the County of Dorset*, vol. 3, pt 1 (1970), pp. 46–8.

## Chapter 3: The Birth of the London Estate, 1755–1823

1 E. Bright Ashford, *Lisson Green: a Domesday Village in St Marylebone* (1960).
2 Ann Saunders, *Regent's Park* (2nd ed., 1981). The total acreage of the Marylebone estate has been variously stated. Archives, ref. P/E/1/11/1 ('A Mapp of Land belonging to Henry William Portman in the Parish of St Marylebon in the County of Middlesex, 1741'), gives a total of 258 acres 1 rood and 23 perches [258.39 acres], divided into two farms, and presumably provides an accurate statement of the acreage in the period just before development began. Smith, p. 39, writing in 1833, says 'about 270 acres'; but in a variant edition (also of 1833), published after he had been given access to an early abstract of title (now untraceable), he says 'about 300 acres'. This higher figure may represent the approximate original area of the estate before Henry VIII took land from it to create Marylebone Park.
3 Archives, ref. P/E 3/2/1.
4 SHC, ref. DD/PM 8/8/1–22.
5 James L. Howgego and Ida Darlington, *Printed Maps of London, 1553–1850* (1978), no. 101/1A ('Plan of London on the Same Scale as Paris').
6 Archives, ref. P/E 1/3/283.

7  K. Melville Poole, *The Portman Estate: A Study in Private Planning* (unpublished thesis, 1952).
8  Eileen Harris, *The Genius of Robert Adam: His Interiors* (2001), pp 296–315.
9  WCA has created a CD containing historic maps of Marylebone.
10 Dan Cruickshank, *The Secret History of Georgian London*, (2009).
11 Smith, p. 153.
12 Two copies of the document (with plans) conveying these sites to the trustees for the new parish church are in Archives, ref. P/E 1/3/255–6.
13 Smith, p. 201.
14 Sonia W. Addis-Smith, 'Porter, David (1746/7–1819)', *ODNB* (2004).
15 The minutes of the Portman Square Garden Trust have survived from its creation in 1782 (Archives, ref. P/E 1/10/1–3) and are described in Todd Longstaffe-Gowan, 'Portman Square Garden: "The Montpelier of England"', *The London Gardener*, vol. 12 (2006–7).
16 Francis Sheppard, *Local Government in St Marylebone 1688–1835* (1958), p. 208.
17 The Survey of London, The French Chapel in Marylebone, (7 September 2018).
18 *The Gentleman's Magazine* (March 1812), p. 286.
19 WCA has created a CD containing historic maps of Marylebone.

**Chapter 4: Family Matters**
1  Archives, ref. P/E 3/1/103.
2  R. G. Thorne, *The History of Parliament: The House of Commons, 1790–1820* (1986), pp. 873–4.
3  Archives, ref. P/E 3/1/3. After deductions of almost £9,000 the amount of tax payable, charged at 10%, was £880.
4  Quoted in Portman, pp. 122–3.
5  Archives, ref. P/E 1/3/46.
6  WCA, ref. D Misc 169/1–5.
7  Archives, ref. P/F 3/87/1.
8  BL, Add Ms 41,567, ff.132–48.
9  R. B. Martin, *Enter Rumour: Four Early Victorian Scandals*, (1962), gives a full account of the Lady Flora Hastings affair.
10 Archives, ref. P/F 8/35–43.
11 Archives, ref. P/F 3/107.
12 BL, Add Ms 44,438, f.75.
13 BL, Add Ms 44,438, f.88.
14 Michael Portman kindly provided the details of this branch of the family.
15 Ian Gaunt and John Tory, *Mary Portman's Violin: Mary Isabel Portman 1877–1931* (Bryanston Village History Group, 2010, rev. 2014).
16 Archives, ref. P/F 3/113/5.

**Chapter 5: Dorset Days**
1  Bateman, p. 365.
2  *Somerset County Gazette*, 18 August 1877.

3 Mayberry, 38–40.
4 Historic England, Listed Building description; L. H. Ruegg, 'Farming of Dorsetshire', *Journal of the Royal Agricultural Society of England*, vol. 15 (1854), 389–454.
5 *Poole and Dorset Herald*, 6 May 1880; H. Rider Haggard, *Rural England* (1906), 265–7.
6 *Poole and Dorset Herald*, 6 May 1880.
7 Reminiscences of R. G. Tapper of Durweston (unpublished, 1972).
8 Forrester, 9 May 1884, 15 May 1888, 14 December 1871, 20 December 1879, 8 January 1891; *Western Gazette*, 15 June 1888.
9 Forrester, 24 December 1883, 11 January 1876, 24 December 1872; *Western Gazette*, 30 December 1898.
10 Forrester, 23 August 1882.
11 Forrester, 24 January 1884.
12 Forrester, 7 August 1877; Mayberry, 43–4.
13 Forrester, 14 April and 25 June 1883, 25 September 1884.
14 Forrester, 19 and 21 November 1888.
15 Forrester, 24 November 1888; *Taunton Courier*, 28 November 1888.
16 Forrester, 6 June and 28 July 1889.
17 *Western Gazette*, 13 March 1896, 7 February 1890.
18 *Western Gazette*, 16 March 1917.
19 Portman, pp. 134–5; *Somerset County Gazette*, 24 November 1888.
20 John Newman and Nikolaus Pevsner, *The Buildings of England: Dorset* (1972), p. 118; Saint, pp. 151 and 327; Portman, pp. 135–6.
21 Andrew Saint, 'Shaw, Richard Norman (1831–1912)', *ODNB* (2007); *Western Gazette*, 26 April 1895.
22 *Western Gazette*, 15 February 1895; Forrester, 17 November 1889, 15 May 1890, 23 December 1892; *Western Gazette*, 26 May 1893; Archives, ref. P/F3/113/1 (letter of Richard Norman Shaw to Lord Portman, 28 March 1889).
23 Forrester, 11 May 1892, 23–4 May, 24 and 27 November 1893.
24 Saint, p. 329.
25 Forrester, 17 June and 22 October 1894, 24 February, 14 March, 28 April and 27 June 1896; Saint, p. 331; *Western Gazette*, 12 August 1898.
26 Forrester, 5 November 1894, 18 April and 23–4 April 1895; *Western Gazette*, 26 April 1895, 14 February and 3 July 1896; *The Times*, 20 June 1896.
27 Reminiscences of R. G. Tapper of Durweston (unpublished, 1972); Bryanston Women's Institute, *History of Bryanston* (nd, *c.* 1933).
28 Archives, ref. P/F 3/118/1 (Bryanston visitors' book); *Western Gazette*, 17 December 1909.
29 Portman, pp. 140–2.
30 Portman, pp. 135–6; *Western Gazette*, 24 October 1919.

**Chapter 6: The Growth of the London Estate, 1824–1919**
1 Walford, vol. 5, p. 254.

2 Smith, pp. 217–8.
3 Walford, vol. 5, p. 259.
4 David Brandon and Alan Brooke, *Marylebone & Tyburn Past* (2007), p. 110.
5 Charles Booth, *Life and Labour of the People in London, Third Series: Religious Influences*, vol. 1 (1902), p. 200.
6 Walford, vol. 4, pp. 419–20.
7 Walford, vol. 4, p. 410.
8 Erica McDonald and David J. Smith, *Pineapples and Pantomimes: A History of Church Street and Lisson Green* (1992), which has provided many details for this chapter.
9 Information on Frederick Hunt was kindly supplied by Brian O'Connell.
10 Archives, ref. P/E 1/14/4/8, and Jonathan Mantle, *The Portman Story, 1846–2001* (2002).
11 Nicola Beauman, *Morgan: A Biography of E. M. Forster* (1993), pp. 4ff.
12 Nicholas Draper and Rachel Evans, 'Mapping slave-ownership on to London and its districts; the Portman estate as a case study', *London Topographical Society Newsletter*, no.77, November 2013 (Legacies of British Slave-ownership project, University College, London).
13 Raymond Lamont-Brown, *Edward VII's Last Loves: Alice Keppel and Agnes Keyser* (1998), p. 86.

## Chapter 7: The Problems Mount

1 *Western Gazette*, 26 January 1923.
2 Forrester, 30 July 1887.
3 *Western Gazette*, 16 July 1897.
4 *Sussex Agricultural Express*, 1 April 1898; Forrester, 9 and 17 January, 19 March, 9 April, 21 July 1897.
5 Portman, p. 135.
6 Forrester, 19 June 1906.
7 *Western Gazette*, 6 November and 4 December 1925; Mayberry, p. 46.
8 See David Cannadine, *The Decline and Fall of the British Aristocracy* (2nd ed., 2005).
9 Information from The Hon. Mrs Rosemary Pease; Mayberry, pp. 44–5; SHC, ref DD/PM.
10 Archives, ref. P/F 3/120/1–6.
11 *Western Gazette*, 13 February 1931.
12 Archives, ref. P/E 1/1/2, p. 104.
13 Archives, ref. P/F 3/120/6.
14 See Roy Berkeley, *A Spy's London* (2nd ed., 2014).

## Chapter 8: The Problems Resolved

1 *Western Gazette*, 7 July 1950.
2 Portman, pp. 95–100.
3 Simon Jenkins, *Landlords to London: The Story of a Capital and its Growth* (1975), chapters 12–14.

4 Richard Davenport-Hines, 'Rayne, Max, Baron Rayne (1918–2003)', *ODNB* (2007); *The Independent*, 12 October 2003.

5 *39–42 Portman Square, City of Westminster: A Standing Building Survey* (Museum of London Archaeology Service, 2004).

6 *Portman Estate Conservation Area Audit* (Westminster City Council, 2003); Bridget Cherry and Nikolaus Pevsner, *The Buildings of England. London 3: North West* (1991), p. 651.

7 Richard Davenport-Hines, *An English Affair: Sex, Class and Power in the Age of Profumo* (2013).

8 Ray Coleman, *Lennon: The Definitive Biography* (1995).

9 Michael Kitson, 'Blunt, Anthony Frederick (1907–1983)', rev. Miranda Carter, *ODNB* (2008); Roy Berkeley, *A Spy's London* (2nd ed., 2014).

10 Brian Brivati, 'Goodman, Arnold Abraham, Baron Goodman (1913–1995), *ODNB* (2004).

11 *The Times*, 18 July 2011.

12 'The Great Estates, Part Four: The Portman Estate', *The London Magazine*, 26 July 2016; *Public Realm Strategy: The Portman Estate* (Gehl Architects, April 2008).

13 'Central London's next regeneration hotspot... 110 acres in Zone 1 set for £240 million transformation', *London Evening Standard*, 13 July 2016.

Thomas Portman of Taunton, fl. 1302
|
William (–c 1413), MP 1362–1406 = Alice Crosse
|
Walter (–c 1456), MP 1417–35 = Christina de Orchard (–c 1472)
|
John, lawyer of the Temple (–c 1486)
|
John, lawyer of the Middle Temple, buried in the Temple Church (–1521)
|
Sir William (c 1498–1557), Lord Chief Justice 1555 = Elizabeth Gilbert

Sir Henry (–1591) = Joan Michell        Mary (1539–1606) = Sir John Stawell

- Elizabeth (1551–) = Thomas Lord Paulet
- Rachel (1554–1631)
- Sir Hugh (1561–1604)
- Sir John 1st Bt (1562–1612) = Anne Gifford (–1638)
- Joan (1566–1633) = Sir John Wyndham

Children of Sir John 1st Bt:
- Joan (1598–1655) = George Speke
- Elizabeth (1604–36) = John Bluett (–1634)
- Sir Henry 2nd Bt (c1595–1621) = Lady Anne Stanley
- Sir John 3rd Bt (1605–24) unm
- Sir Hugh 4th Bt (1607–29) unm
- Sir William 5th Bt (1608–45) = Anne Colles (–1651)
- Grace (1601–61)

George    Philippa = Edward Berkeley of Pylle
                    | (–1699)
          Edward = Elizabeth Ryves
          (–1707)  (–1724)

Sir William 6th Bt (1644–90)
= (1) Elizabeth Cutler (–1673)
  (2) Elizabeth Southcote (–1680)
  (3) Mary Holman (–1689)
No issue

Anne
(1610–95)
= Sir Edward
Seymour
3$^{rd}$ Bt (1610–88)

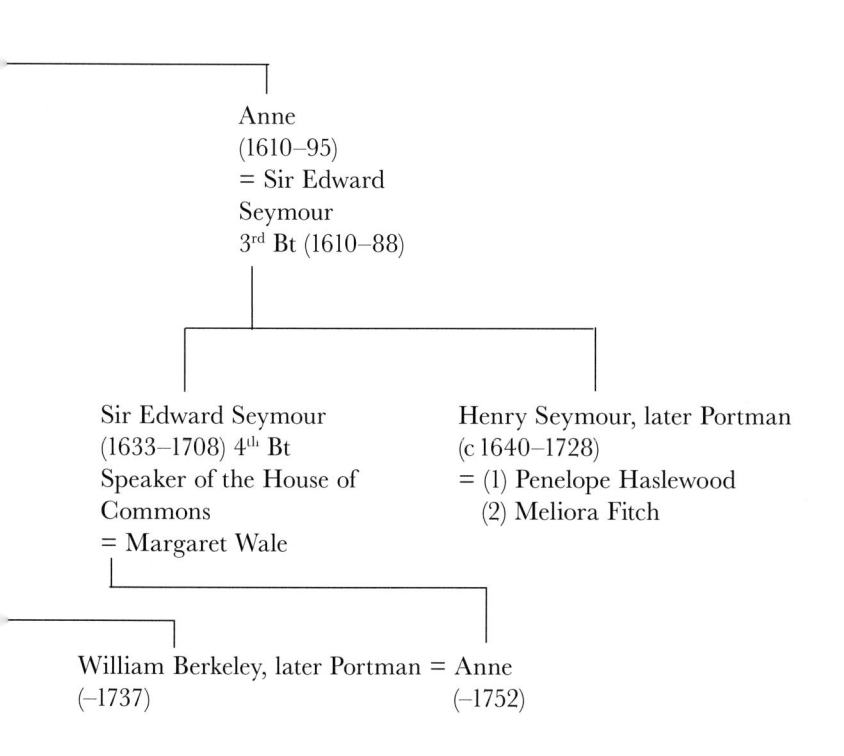

Sir Edward Seymour　　　　Henry Seymour, later Portman
(1633–1708) 4$^{th}$ Bt　　　　(c 1640–1728)
Speaker of the House of　　= (1) Penelope Haslewood
Commons　　　　　　　　　(2) Meliora Fitch
= Margaret Wale

William Berkeley, later Portman = Anne
(–1737)　　　　　　　　　　　　(–1752)

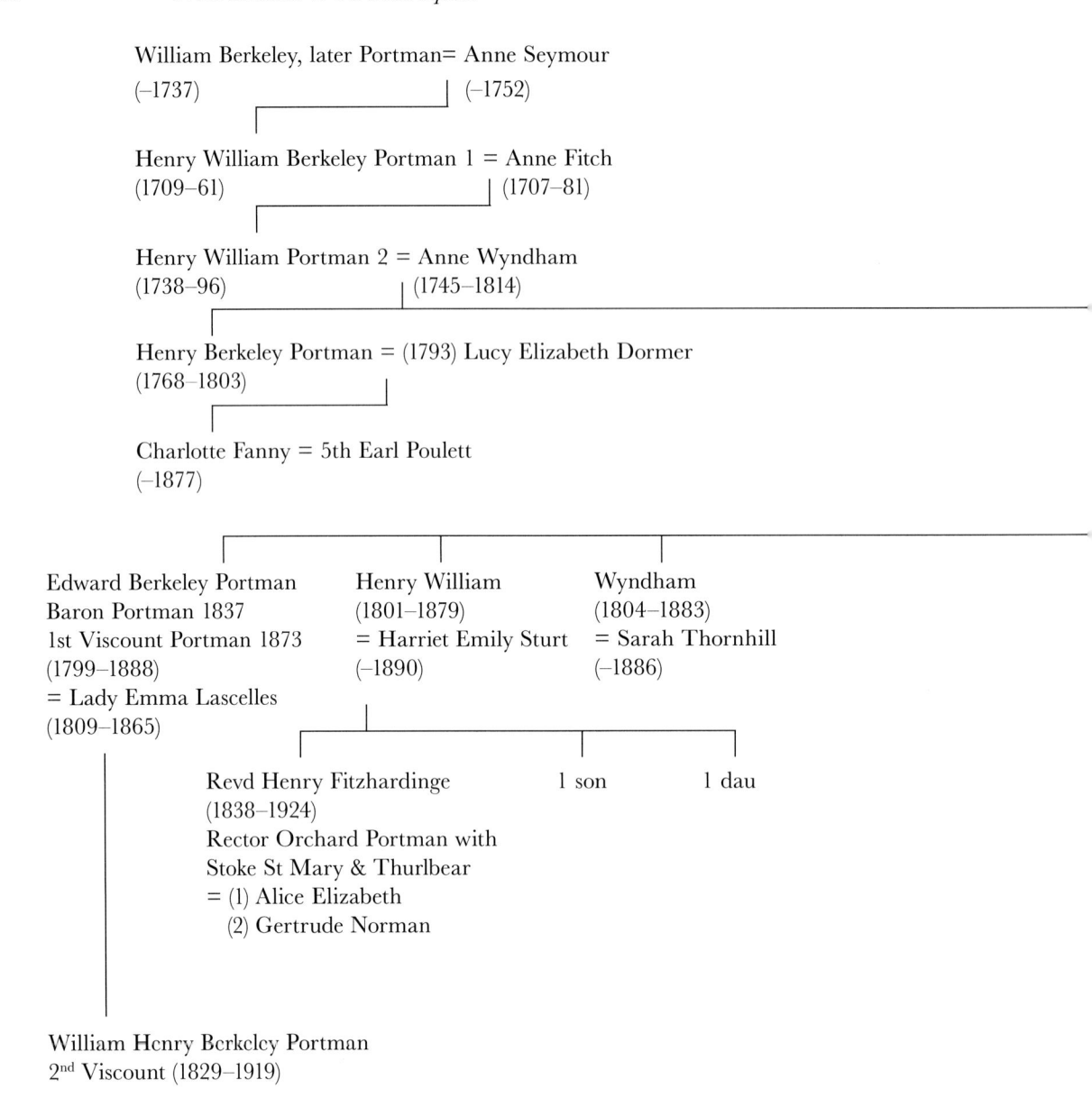

William Berkeley, later Portman = Anne Seymour
(–1737) (–1752)

Henry William Berkeley Portman 1 = Anne Fitch
(1709–61) (1707–81)

Henry William Portman 2 = Anne Wyndham
(1738–96) (1745–1814)

Henry Berkeley Portman = (1793) Lucy Elizabeth Dormer
(1768–1803)

Charlotte Fanny = 5th Earl Poulett
(–1877)

Edward Berkeley Portman    Henry William         Wyndham
Baron Portman 1837         (1801–1879)           (1804–1883)
1st Viscount Portman 1873  = Harriet Emily Sturt = Sarah Thornhill
(1799–1888)                (–1890)               (–1886)
= Lady Emma Lascelles
(1809–1865)

                           Revd Henry Fitzhardinge      1 son    1 dau
                           (1838–1924)
                           Rector Orchard Portman with
                           Stoke St Mary & Thurlbear
                           = (1) Alice Elizabeth
                             (2) Gertrude Norman

William Henry Berkeley Portman
2nd Viscount (1829–1919)

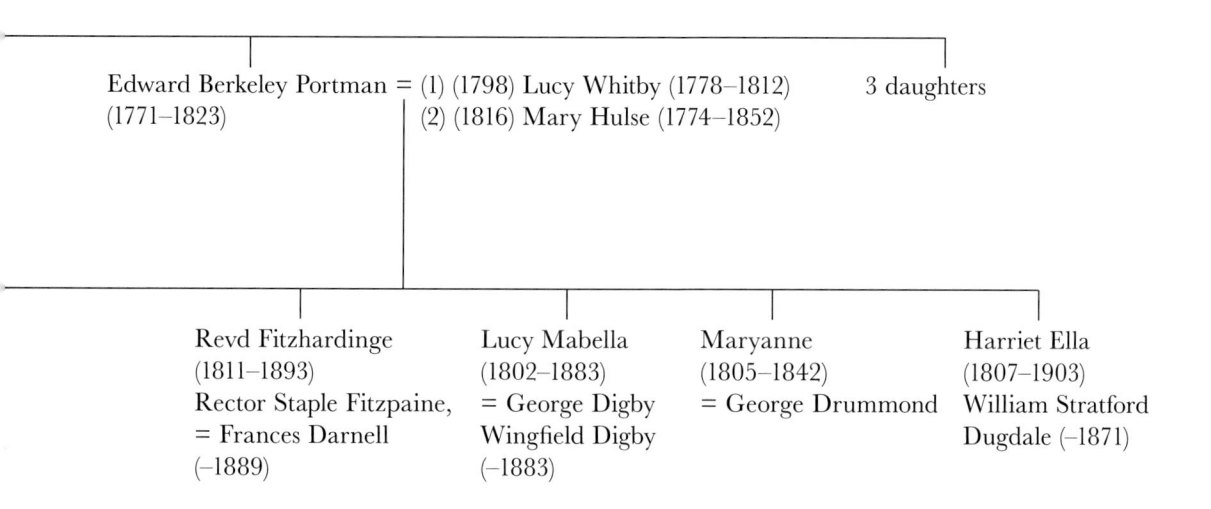

Edward Berkeley Portman = (1) (1798) Lucy Whitby (1778–1812)   3 daughters
(1771–1823)                (2) (1816) Mary Hulse (1774–1852)

Revd Fitzhardinge        Lucy Mabella         Maryanne             Harriet Ella
(1811–1893)              (1802–1883)          (1805–1842)          (1807–1903)
Rector Staple Fitzpaine, = George Digby       = George Drummond    William Stratford
= Frances Darnell        Wingfield Digby                           Dugdale (–1871)
(–1889)                  (–1883)

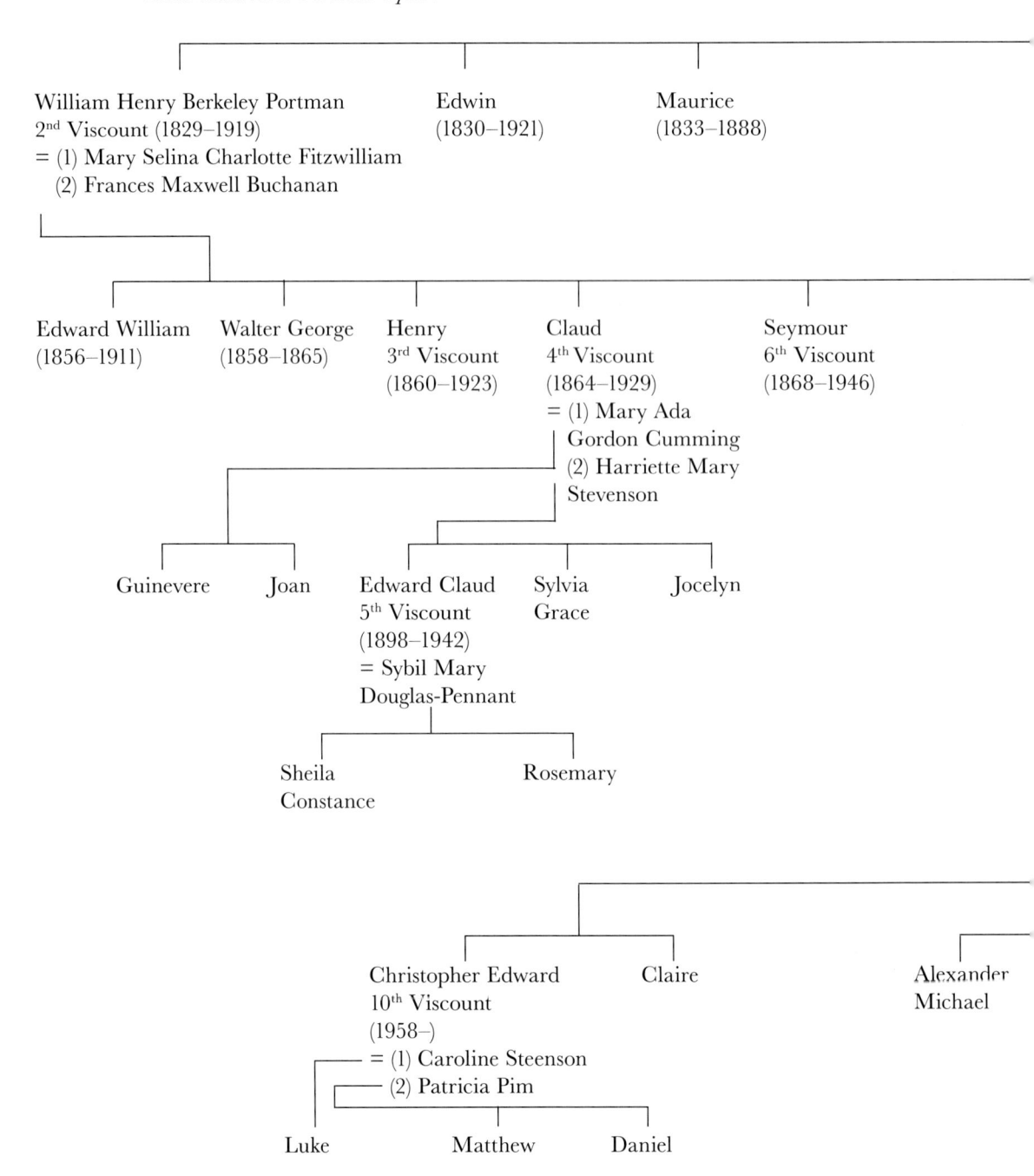

*From Somerset to Portman Square*

- **William Henry Berkeley Portman**
  2nd Viscount (1829–1919)
  = (1) Mary Selina Charlotte Fitzwilliam
    (2) Frances Maxwell Buchanan
- **Edwin** (1830–1921)
- **Maurice** (1833–1888)

Children:
- **Edward William** (1856–1911)
- **Walter George** (1858–1865)
- **Henry** 3rd Viscount (1860–1923)
- **Claud** 4th Viscount (1864–1929)
  = (1) Mary Ada Gordon Cumming
    (2) Harriette Mary Stevenson
- **Seymour** 6th Viscount (1868–1946)

Children of Henry: Guinevere, Joan

Children of Claud:
- **Edward Claud** 5th Viscount (1898–1942)
  = Sybil Mary Douglas-Pennant
- Sylvia Grace
- Jocelyn

Children of Edward Claud: Sheila Constance, Rosemary

- **Christopher Edward** 10th Viscount (1958–)
  = (1) Caroline Steenson
    (2) Patricia Pim
- Claire
- Alexander Michael

Children of Christopher Edward: Luke, Matthew, Daniel

Family Trees 183

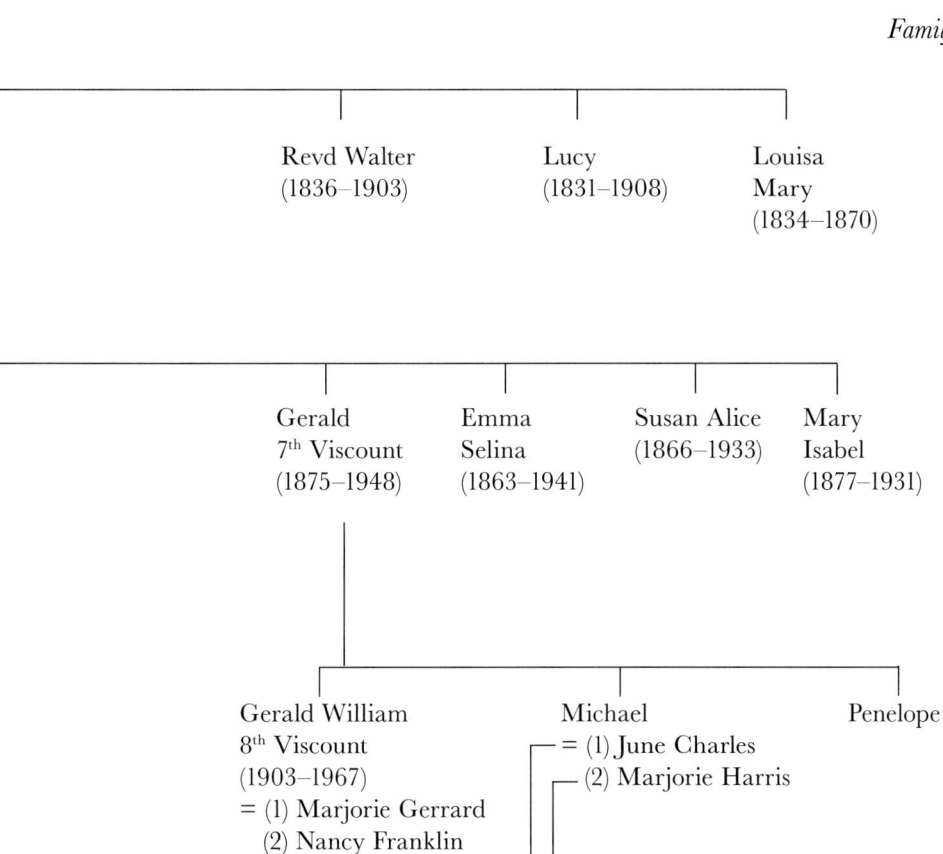

Revd Walter (1836–1903) | Lucy (1831–1908) | Louisa Mary (1834–1870)

Gerald 7th Viscount (1875–1948) | Emma Selina (1863–1941) | Susan Alice (1866–1933) | Mary Isabel (1877–1931)

Gerald William 8th Viscount (1903–1967)
= (1) Marjorie Gerrard
  (2) Nancy Franklin

Michael
= (1) June Charles
  (2) Marjorie Harris

Penelope

Edward Henry 9th Viscount (1934–1999)
= (1) Rosemary Farris
  (2) Penelope Allin

Davina

Michael William

Suna

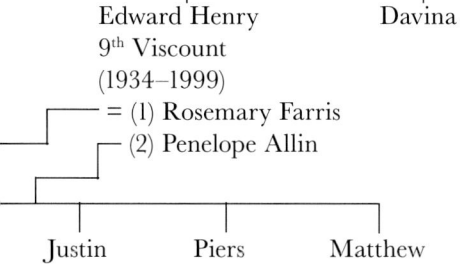

Justin | Piers | Matthew

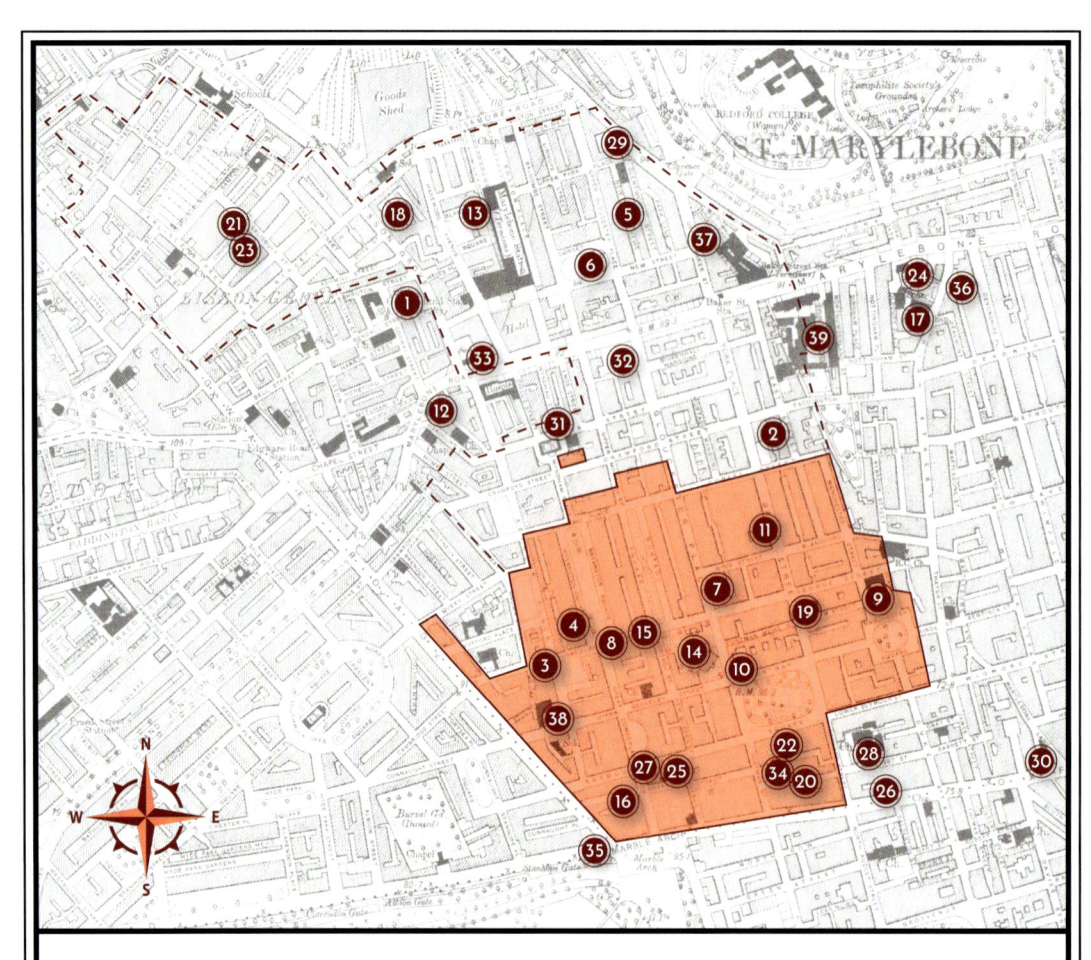

**MAP SHOWING THE LOCATION OF KEY SITES ON THE LONDON ESTATE, DEPICTED ON 1885 ORDNANCE SURVEY MAP**

▇ Current Estate
┆ Pre 1952 Estate

1. The Baker family's estate
2. 64 Baker Street, SOE HQ
3. Bryanston Court
4. Bryanston Square, site of former Portman family home
5. Clarence Gate Mansions
6. Dorset Square, site of the original Lord's Cricket Ground
7. Site of French Chapel Royal
8. 68 Great Cumberland Place, former family office
9. Hertford House (Wallace Collection)
10. Home House
11. Site of Life Guards Barracks, later the Baker Street Bazaar
12. Site of Lilestone Manor House & later Queen Charlotte's hospital
13. Marylebone Station
14. Site of Montagu House, later Portman House
15. 12 Montagu Street, former family office
16. Site of Odeon Cinema, Marble Arch
17. Site of old parish church, c. 1400
18. Site of Portman Buildings
19. Site of Portman Chapel
20. Site of Portman Foot Barracks
21. Site of Portman Market
22. 40 Portman Square, current Estate office
23. Site of Portman Theatre
24. Present St Marylebone Parish Church, 1817
25. Quebec Chapel, later Church of the Annunciation
26. Selfridges
27. Seymour Street, former Estate office
28. Somerset Street
29. St Cyprian's Church
30. Site of St John's Parish Church, c. 1200
31. St Mary's Church, Bryanston Square
32. St Marylebone Council House
33. St Marylebone Grammar School
34. Three Tuns Public House
35. Site of Tyburn Gallows
36. Site of Tyburn Manor House
37. 27 Upper Baker Street, former family office
38. West London Synagogue
39. Site of Workhouse

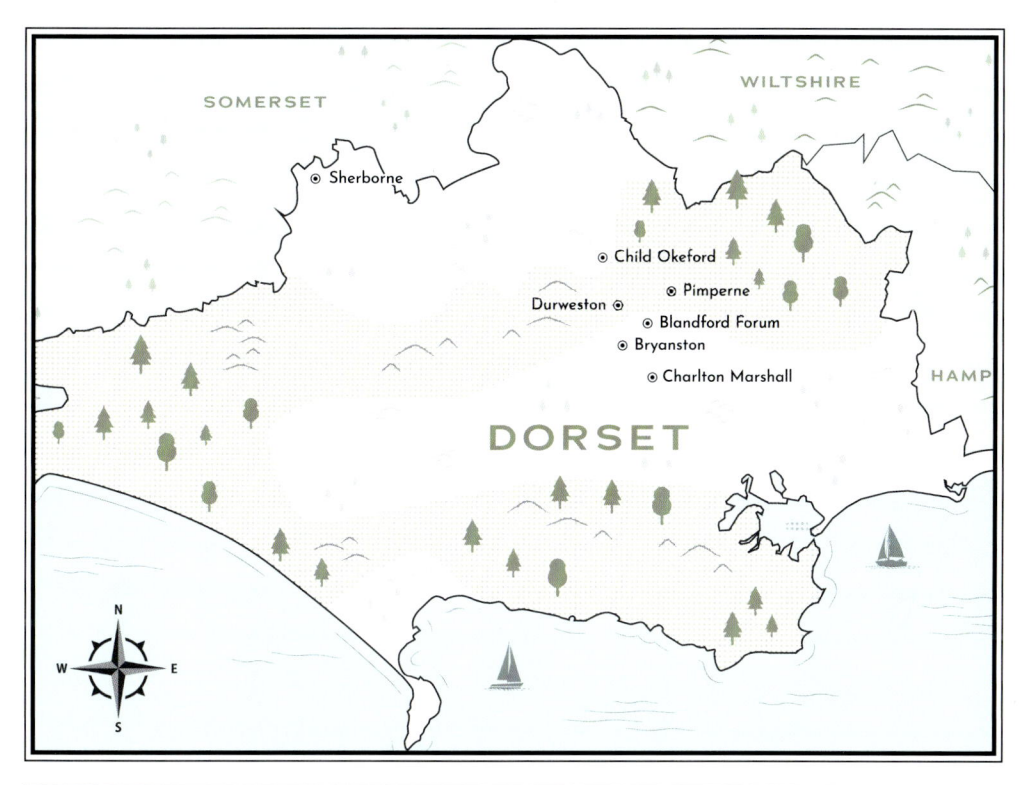

Maps   185

## Dorset

- Sherborne
- Child Okeford
- Durweston
- Pimperne
- Blandford Forum
- Bryanston
- Charlton Marshall

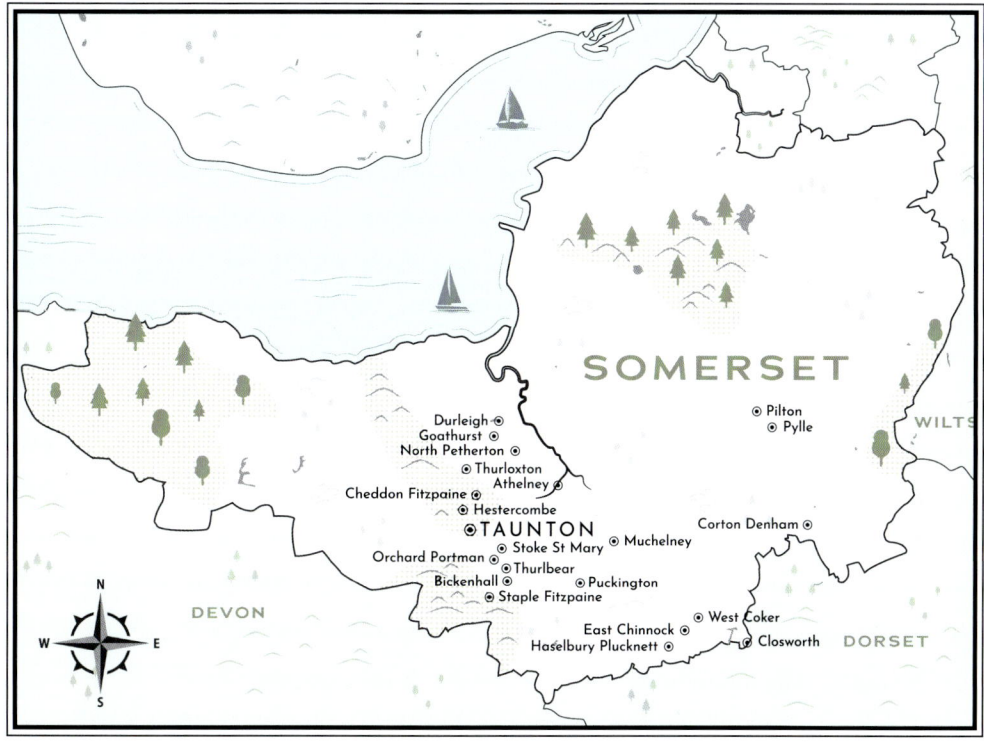

## Somerset

- Durleigh
- Goathurst
- North Petherton
- Thurloxton
- Athelney
- Cheddon Fitzpaine
- Hestercombe
- TAUNTON
- Orchard Portman
- Stoke St Mary
- Muchelney
- Bickenhall
- Thurlbear
- Puckington
- Staple Fitzpaine
- Pilton
- Pylle
- Corton Denham
- East Chinnock
- West Coker
- Haselbury Plucknett
- Closworth

# Index

Ackermann, Rudolph 66
Adam, Robert 61
Adams, Abraham 61
Adams, Samuel 61
Alleine, Joseph 29
Armstrong, Eliza 115
Ashmill Street (London) 113
Athelney Abbey (Somerset) 17
Austen, Jane 62
Axe, Thomas 28, 29, 30, 35, 171n2

Babbage, Charles 126
Baker, Peter William 62, 68
Baker Street (London) 62, 118–119, *126*–127, 142, 144–145, *150*, 161–162
Baker Street Station 122, 129, 143
Baker, William 55–56, 57, 58, 62, 72
Banfield, Frank 124
Batt, Richard 23
Battle of Naseby (1645) 24–25
Battle of Sedgmoor 31
Bedford Square (London) 61
Beerbohm, Max 150–151
Bennett, Arnold 151
Berkeley, Anne 38–39
Berkeley, Edward (–1699) 39–40, *40*
Berkeley, Sir Maurice 40
Berkeley, William *see* Portman, William Berkeley

Betjeman, John 123
Bickenhall (Somerset) 17
Birley, Oswald 138
Blackamore, James 19, 20, 170n9
Blake, Robert 23–24
Blandford Square (London) 112, 122
Blenerhasset, Joan 51–52
Blenerhasset, John 51–52, 55
'block' building 116, 117
Bloomsbury (London) 58
Bluett, Elizabeth *see* Portman, Elizabeth (1604–1636)
Bluett, John (–1634) 20, 21
Blunt, Anthony 55, 158–159
Bolivar, Simon 127
Booth, Charles 116–117
Bower, Catherine 78
Bowles, Margaret 46, 173n26
Bowles, William 46, 173n26
Brock, Tony 159–160
Brunswick Chapel (Upper Berkeley Street, London) 67–68
Bryanston House (Dorset) 27, 38, 40, 45–*50*, 61, 91, 93–100
 rebuilding 100–109, 124
 sale 134–135, 153
Bryanston Square (London) 63, 68, 75, 78, 79, 90, 111, 145, *146*, 158
Buck, George 58, 68, 69
Buck, James 58

Bulwer-Lytton, Edward 126–127
Buxted Park (East Sussex) 131, *133*
Buyse, Anton 31–33

Calmel Buildings 64–65
Charles I, 22–23, 24–25
Charles II, 27, 29–33
Charles Street (London) 115
Cheddon Fitzpaine (Somerset) 131, 135
Child Okeford (Dorset) 132, 133
Chiltern Street (Marylebone) 125, 143, 161
Church Street (Marylebone) 145, 148
Clark, Sir James 83–84
Clavelshays (Somerset) 17
Clutton, Gareth 160
Colles, Anne *see* Portman, Anne (née Colles)
Colles, Captain Humphrey 29
Collins, Wilkie 126
Comper, Sir Ninian 120
Cooper, Sir Anthony Ashley 23–24
Cooper, Sir Edwin 141
Cosway, Richard 62
Cosway Street (London) 119–120
Courtauld, Samuel 59
Covent Garden (London) 58
Cutler, Elizabeth *see* Portman, Elizabeth (née Cutler)

Deighton, Len 122
dissolution of the monasteries 17, 54
Dormer, Lucy Elizabeth *see* Portman, Lucy Elizabeth (née Dormer)
Dorset Square (London) 63, 68, 72, 73, 111–112, 123–124, 148
Douglas-Pennant, Sybil Mary *see* Portman, Sybil Mary (née Douglas-Pennant)
Dowdney, George 125
Dunwear (Somerset) 17
Durleigh (Somerset) 17
Durweston (Dorset) 94, 96, 107, 109, *155*

Edgware Road (London) 52, *54*, 112, 142
Edward VI 17
Edward VII 97, 108, 128, 144
Eliot, George 126
Eliot, T.S. 151
Elliott, John 39
Elwes, John 62
English Civil War (1642–1651) 22–25

Fancourt, Edward 81–82
Faraday, Michael 126
Farrant, Amy 31
Fenn-Smith, Oliver 160
Fitch, Ann *see* Portman, Ann (née Fitch)
Fitch, Meliora *38*
Fitzwilliam, Mary Selina Charlotte *see* Portman, Mary Selina Charlotte (née Fitzwilliam)
Forrester, James 96–*97*, 99
Forrester, Julia *96*–100, 105, 106–107, 133
Forster, E.M. 127
Franklin, Nancy *see* Portman, Nancy (née Franklin)
French Chapel Royal (Little George Street, London) 71–72, 127
Frere, Emma Andalusia *see* Portman, Emma Andalusia (née Frere)
Furmedge, J.H. 139–140, 144, 147

Garret Anderson, Elizabeth 126
George Street (London) 120, 127
George V 108
Gerrard, Marjorie *see* Portman, Marjorie (née Gerrard)
Gibbon, Edward 42–43
Gibson, Frank 160
Gilbert, Elizabeth *see* Portman, Elizabeth (née Gilbert)
Gillett, Edward 147, 157, 159, 160
Gissing, George 150–151
Gladstone, William Ewart 84–85, 97, 116

Glorious Revolution 34
Gloucester Place (London) 162
Glyn, George 85
Goathurst (Somerset) 17
Goodman, Lord 160
Gordon-Cumming, Mary Ada *see* Portman, Mary Ada (née Gordon-Cumming)
Goring, George, Lord 24
Grabham, Andrew 136–137
Great Cumberland Place (London) 62–63, 119, 121, 126, 145, *146*
Grenville, Sir Richard 24
Guy, George 100

Halley, Edmund 27–28
Hampden Gurney, Revd John 121
Hampden Gurney Street (London) 121
Harcourt Street (London) 65–66
Hardwick, Philip 122–123, 126
Hardwick, Philip Charles 122–123
Hardwick, Thomas 119–120, 122
Harewood Square (London) 112, 122
Harris, Marjorie *see* Portman, Marjorie (née Harris)
Haslewood, Penelope *see* Portman, Penelope (née Haslewood)
Hastings, Flora 83–84
Hatherell, Charles 160
Haydn, Josef 72
Haydon, Benjamin 127
Healing Manor (Lincolnshire) 138
Henry VIII 54–55
Hestercombe House (Somerset) *95*, *98*–99, 131, 132
Hill, Octavia 115–116
Hobsbawm, Professor Eric 122
Hobson, Thomas 51
Hogarth, William 65
Holcombe Rogus (Devon) 20–*21*
Holman, Mary *see* Portman, Mary (née Holman)
Home, Elizabeth (Countess of Home) 61

Home House (Portman Square, London) *59*, *60*, 158
Hooke, Robert 27–28
Hooper, Henry 36
Hopton, Sir Ralph 23
Horwood, Richard 62–64
Hulse, Mary *see* Portman, Mary (née Hulse)
Hunt, Frederick 115, 116, 123–124

Inverinate (Scotland) 138–139, 162

James II 30, 33
Jekyll, Gertrude 99
Jenkins, Thomas 72
Jermyn Street (London) 65
Jerome, Jerome K. 122
Jones, Inigo 58

Keeler, Christine 158
Keppel, Alice 108, 128, 144
Kew Palace (London) 19–20
Kip, Johannes 19, 45
Kneller, Sir Godfrey 38
Knighton House (Dorset) *94*, 134, 138, 153
Knyff, Leonard 18–19, 42, 45, 170n9

Lascelles, Lady Emma *see* Portman, Lady Emma (née Lascelles)
Lay, Richard 160
Lear, Edward 126
leasehold system (18th century) 58, 115, 124
Lessey, Revd Thomas 29
Lilestone Manor (London) 51–52, 53, *54*–55
Linley, Elizabeth 62
Linnell, John 127
Lisson Green (London) 56, 69
Lisson Grove (London) 62, 72, *112*, *113*–117, 127, 141
Lisson Road (London) 122
London Estate *see* Marylebone
Lord, Thomas 72, 73–74

Lower, Richard 34
Lumley, Lord Richard 31, 33
Lutyens, Sir Edwin 99

Macaulay, Rose 151
Maiden Bradley (Wiltshire) *35*
Mallack, John 29
Manchester Square (London) 62, 111, 117, 158
mansion flats 125, 143–144
Marble Arch Station (London) 122
Marchaunt, William 15
Marylebone 51–57, 69–70, 163
   development 51–75
   growth (1824–1919) 111–129
   transport infrastructure 122
Marylebone Road (London) 122, 148
   *see also* New Road (London)
Maugham, Somerset 151
Meacher, Higgins and Thomas Pharmacy (London) 66
Millington, Thomas 34
Mills, Bertram 122
Monmouth, Duke of 29–33
Montagu, Mrs Elizabeth 55, 61–62
Montagu House (Portman Square) 90–*91*, 138, *145*
Montagu Mews (London) *127*
Montagu Square (London) 62, 63, 68, 111, 158
Montez, Lola 127
Moore, Bill 160
Mordaunt, Lady 28
Muchelney Abbey (Somerset) 20
Musgrave, George 35

New Quebec Street (London) 161
New Road (later Marylebone Road, London) 62–64, 68, 70, 111–*112*
North Petherton (Somerset) 17

Old Quebec Street (London) 65, 142
Orchard, Christina de *see* Portman, Christina (née de Orchard)
Orchard House (Orchard Portman, Somerset) *18*–19, *20*, 24
Orchard Portman (Somerset) 16, 17, 24–25, 29, 42, 131
Orchard, Richard de 16
Orchard Street (London) 56, 62, 64–65
Oxford Street (London) 52, *54*, 56, 61, 65, 125, 142

Palmer, Samuel 127
Park Road (London) 120
Parkin, Henry 33
Parkinson, James Thompson 75, 78–80, 113
Penfold Street (Marylebone) *125*
Pepys, Samuel 28, 29
Pevsner, Nikolaus 101, 173n31
Pitt, William (the younger) 126–127
Porter, David 62, 68
Portman, Ann (née Fitch) 41, *43*
Portman, Anne (1610–1695) 20, 40, 178
Portman, Anne (Berkeley Portman) 39–40, 178–179
Portman, Anne Mary 78
Portman, Lady Anne (née Colles; –1651) 24, 178
Portman, Anne (née Wyndham) 42
Portman, Arthur 88
Portman, Berkeley 160
Portman Burtley Estate (Buckinghamshire) 147, 149, 162
Portman Chapel (Baker Street, later St Paul's Church) 67–68
Portman Chapel (Bryanston, Dorset) 153–*154*
Portman, Christina (née de Orchard) 16–17
Portman, Christopher Edward Berkeley (**10th Viscount**) 160, *161*
Portman, Claud Berkeley (**4th Viscount**; 1864–1929) 90, 132–*136*, 182
Portman, Dorothy Marie Isolde (née Sheffield) 138–*139*

Portman, Edward Berkeley (1771–1823) 70, 74–75, 77–81
Portman, Edward Berkeley II (**1st Viscount**; 1799–1888) 81–91, 93–100, *97*, 111, 121, 124–125, 131, 132, 180
Portman, Edward Claud 'Eddie' (**5th Viscount**; 1898–1942) 132, 135–*137*, 147, 182
Portman, Edward Henry Berkeley (**9th Viscount**; 1934–1999) 155–*156*, 157, 160, 162, 182
Portman, Edward William 'Teddy' (1856–1911) 89–90, *97*–99, 131, *132*, 135, 182
Portman, Edwin Berkeley (1830–1921) 86–87
Portman, Elizabeth (1604–1636) 20, 21, 178
Portman, Elizabeth (née Cutler; –1673) 29, 180
Portman, Elizabeth (née Gilbert) 55
Portman, Elizabeth (née Southcote; –1680) 29
Portman, Emma Andalusia (née Frere) 131
Portman, Lady Emma (née Lascelles) 82–84
Portman, Revd Fitzhardinge Berkeley (1811–1893) *87*, 136
Portman, Emma Selina (1863–1941) 91, 182
Portman Foot Barracks (London) 57–58
Portman, Captain Gerald Berkeley (**7th Viscount**; 1874–1948) 132, *138*–140, 147, 153, 162
Portman, Gerald William (**8th Viscount**; 1903–1967) 138, 148–*149*, 153–155, 182
Portman, Guinevere 132, 182
Portman, Sir Henry (–1591) 19
Portman, Sir Henry (2nd Bt; c 1595–1621) 178

Portman, Henry Berkeley (**3rd Viscount**; 1860–1923) 89–90, 131–132, 182
Portman, Henry Berkeley (1768–1803) 70, 77, 78
Portman, Henry Seymour (c 1640–1728) 34–39, 172n18
Portman, Henry William Berkeley (1801–1879) 87, 180
Portman, Henry William I (1709–1761) 40–41, 55–56, 57
Portman, Henry William II (1738–1796) 41–43, *44*, 45–46, 61, 66–67, 70, 77, 78, 180
Portman, Sir Hugh (4th Bt; 1607–1629) 36–37, 178
Portman, Sir Hugh (1561–1604) 19–20
Portman, Joan (1566–1633) 178
Portman, Joan (1598–1655) 20, 178
Portman, John (–c 1486) 17
Portman, John (–c 1521) 17, 19
Portman, Sir John (1st Bt; 1562–1612) 19–20, 34, 40
Portman, Sir John (3rd Bt; 1605–1624) 20, *22*
Portman, Lucy Elizabeth (née Dormer) 77
Portman, Lucy (née Whitby) 77
Portman, Marjorie (née Gerrard) 148–*149*
Portman, Marjorie (née Harris) 153–155
Portman Market (London) 117–*118*
Portman, Mary Ada (née Gordon-Cumming) 132–133
Portman, Mary Isabel *88*–89, 140, 183
Portman, Mary (née Holman) 29
Portman, Mary (née Hulse) 80, 180
Portman, Mary Selina Charlotte (née Fitzwilliam) 86, 100–*101*, 107, 109, 182
Portman, Maurice Berkeley 87
Portman, Maurice Vidal 88

Portman, Meliora (née Fitch) 38, 39, 41, 172n16
Portman, Michael 138, 183
Portman, Michael Berkeley (1906–1959) 153–156
Portman, Nancy (née Franklin) 155, 182
Portman, Penelope 140
Portman, Penelope (née Haslewood) 38
Portman, Rosemary 136, 182
Portman, Seymour Berkeley (**6th Viscount**; 1868–1946) 137–138, 147, 153
Portman, Sheila Constance 136, 182
Portman Square (London) 55, *58*, 61–68, 73, 111, 145, 150, 157–158, 160–161
Portman Street (London) 56
Portman, Susan Alice (1866–1933) 91, 183
Portman, Sybil Mary (née Douglas-Pennant) 136–*137*
Portman, Thomas (fl 1302) 14
Portman, Walter (–c 1456) 15–17
Portman, Revd Walter Berkeley 87, 88
Portman, William (–c 1413) 15
Portman, Sir William (5th Bt; 1608–1645) 22–25, 27–28, 137
Portman, Sir William (6th Bt; 1644–1690) 15, 19–20, 24–25, 27–29, 34–37, 39–40, 171n17, 172n16
Monmouth Rebellion 29–33, 171n17
Portman, Sir William Berkeley (–1737) 34–35, 39–40, 41
Portman, Sir William (c 1498–1557) *17*–19, 52, 53, 163
Portman, William Henry Berkeley (**2nd Viscount**; 1829–1919) 86, 91, *97*, 100–109, 111, 132–133, 141, 180, 182
Portman, Wyndham Berkeley (1804–1883) 87

Prinsep, William 121
Profumo, John 158
Pylle (Somerset) *41*

Quebec Chapel (Bryanston Street, London, later Church of the Annunciation) 67–68, *71*, 120–121
Quebec Street (London) 57

Rayne, Max 157
Regent's Canal (London) 73–75, 112
Regent's Park (London) 126
Rice-Davies, Mandy 158
Rider Haggard, Henry 95
Rocque, John 56–57
Rothschild, Sir Evelyn de 160

Saint, Andrew 101–102
St Cyprian's (Clarence Gate, London) 120, 121
St Marylebone 51–57, 69–70
St Mary's (Bryanston Square, London) 119, 120, *121*
St Matthew's Church (Penfold Street, London) *118*
Schnebblie, Robert 118
Scrymgeour, W.H. 125
Seaborn, Hugh 160
Seacole, Mary 127
Selfridge, Harry Gordon 56, 125, 142, 143
Seven Years' War 55
Seymour, Anne *see* Portman, Anne (Seymour)
Seymour, Sir Edward (1610–1688) 20, 178
Seymour, Sir Edward (1633–1708) 29, 34, *35*, 37, 178
Seymour, Henry *see* Portman, Henry Seymour
Seymour Place (Marylebone) 122, 142, 149, 161
Seymour Street (Marylebone) 145, *146*, 149

Shaw, Richard Norman 102–106, 173n31
Sheffield, Dorothy Marie Isolde *see* Portman, Dorothy Marie Isolde (née Sheffield)
Sherborne House (Dorset) 38, *39*
Sherbrooke, Revd Neville 124
Sheridan, Richard Brinsley 62
Sherlock Holmes 128–129
Shillibeer, George 122
Siddons, Sarah 126, 127
Simpson, Wallis 144
Smirke, Robert 119
Smith, Thomas 81, 114, 173n2
Snow, C.P. 150–151
Somerset Street (Marylebone) 142–143
Southcote, Elizabeth *see* Portman, Elizabeth (née Southcote)
Southcott, Joanna 127
Speke, Charles 33
Speke, George 20, 29, 30, 34
Speke, Hugh 29
Speke, Joan *see* Portman, Joan (1598–1655)
Speke, Philippa 39–40
Staple Fitzpaine (Somerset) 19–20, 25, 87, 136, 137
Stead, W.T. 115
Stevenson, Harriette Mary 132
Stoke St Mary (Somerset) *86*
Stourton, Sir John 16
Stuart, James 'Athenian' 61
Stubbs, George 62
Summerson, Sir John 55

Tapper, Sir Walter 121
Taunton Priory (Somerset) *14*, 15–16, 17
Taunton (Somerset) 13–15, 17, 27, 34, 162
Thatcher, Margaret 158–159
Thornhill, Sir James 38
Thurloxton (Somerset) 19
Trepplin, E.H. 139
Trollope, Anthony 126
Tussaud, Madame 118–119, 123
Tyburn Manor (London) 51–55, *54–55*

Upper Berkeley Street (London) 120

Vaughan, Sir Henry 24
Victoria, Queen 82–84

Wadham College (Oxford) 20
Ward, Sir Leslie 109
Wells, H.G. 151
West Coker Manor (Somerset) 38
West, Rebecca 151
Whitby, Lucy *see* Portman, Lucy (née Whitby)
White, John 80
Wigmore Street (London) 51
Wilcove Place (London) *124*
William of Orange 34
Wilson, Thomas 68, 122
Wyatt, James 46–47, 48, 61
Wyndham, Anne *see* Portman, Anne (née Wyndham)
Wyndham, Colonel Edmund 23–24
Wyndham, Joan *see* Portman, Joan
Wyndham, Sir John 178
Wythe, John 160

York Street (Marylebone) 125